BIG
IDEAS

FOR LITTLE BOOKS

BIG IDEAS
FOR LITTLE BOOKS

Using Children's Books as a Fun Way to Introduce
Literary Concepts in the Secondary Classroom

SHEVONNE M. ELLIOTT & DAWN S. LAFLEUR

iUniverse, Inc.
Bloomington

Big Ideas for Little Books
Using Children's Books as a Fun Way to Introduce Literary Concepts in the Secondary Classroom

iUniverse books may be ordered through booksellers or by contacting:

iUniverse
1663 Liberty Drive
Bloomington, IN 47403
www.iuniverse.com
1-800-Authors (1-800-288-4677)

ISBN: 978-1-4620-2948-8 (sc)
ISBN: 978-1-4620-2949-5 (ebk)

Library of Congress Control Number: 2011913040

Printed in the United States of America

iUniverse rev. date: 09/12/2011

Acknowledgements

To my family, for always making me believe that I would succeed in whatever I chose to pursue. Thank you, Michael, for always standing silently and solidly behind me, holding me up when I thought I would fall.
—Shevonne

For my husband, Dennis, who has always cheered me on and supported my endeavors. Thank you for never doubting that this book would happen.
—Dawn

Contents

Introduction

Between us, Dawn and I have thirty years of experience in education, spanning all secondary grades and academic levels. We both strive to be life-long learners and use reflective practice to hone our craft. We enjoy trying to new things to engage our students.

One of the new things I decided to try was to use "story time" to introduce a writing style my students had been hearing about since elementary school: persuasive writing. I read them a story called *Earrings!* by Judith Viorst, which is about the lengths a little girl is willing to go to in order to get her first pair of earrings. It was funny and short enough to keep my students' interest. After reading the story, I asked them to think about a time when they went overboard to get their parents to buy them something they really wanted. They were hooked!

The students loved the fact that I read to them "in character," and they were able to relate what they heard to what we were getting ready to do for the lesson. We discussed all the different "tricks" that crafty youngsters use to get what they want. We were able to challenge the effectiveness of one particular technique over the other. In other words, they immediately embraced the ideas I'd introduced using a children's book! Furthermore, they were able to transfer the knowledge they obtained during the lesson to the newer, more involved concept that we were about to explore.

That is what this entire book does for teachers with all levels of experience. These forty-five lessons are a great way to introduce students to the "Big Idea" of a learning unit on a smaller scale. We have chosen the books and the area of concentration for the lessons. All that's required is a little preparation and a lot of enthusiasm!
—Shevonne

How to Use This Book

Our main objective in crafting *Big Ideas for Little Books* was to create a teacher-friendly resource that helps secondary students understand challenging concepts. We hope you, the teacher, will find the lesson ideas presented here practical, easy to implement, and engaging for your students. We want your students to be enthusiastic and interested in learning. We have provided concrete lesson plans for each area of study as well as ideas for extending the learning. In addition, graphic organizers and other handouts accompany the lessons. If you have any questions or need teaching resources, visit our website: www.bigideasforteachers.com.

With just a quick glance, you'll notice that each lesson plan follows the same layout. Here's what you can expect for each lesson:
- the topic(s) the lesson addresses
- a learning objective for the lesson
- the title and author of the book
- a quick overview of the book and how it can be used in your classroom
- a list of the materials you will need
- step-by-step procedures for the lesson
- ideas for extension

We recommend that you do not move chronologically through the book, teaching every lesson in the order it's presented. Rather, use it as a resource, a tool for your teaching kit. As you map out your instructional unit, visit the table of contents to see which lessons relate to the topics in the unit. Read those lessons thoroughly, and make minor adjustments as necessary to reflect your classroom dynamics, teaching style, and other instructional resources.

If you're not sure what you're looking for, flip through the book and scan all the lesson topics and learning objectives. Perhaps you'll get some ideas and clarity about how to approach an instructional unit. We worked diligently to keep the procedures concise and practical, so please don't feel overwhelmed by the thought of taking a new approach to an old lesson.

We hope you find this book useful and invigorating. May it bring an energy and sense of novelty to your classroom that excites both you and your students every day.

Argumentation

At the end of this lesson, students should be able to identify and create logical appeals and fallacies within a text.

Bikes for Rent by Isaac Olaleye

Bikes for Rent not only entertains children, it provides them with a bit of background information about a foreign country (Nigeria). This story provides teachers with a wonderful opportunity to teach about argument and appeals as we explore a question that is becoming more and more important in today's society: should children have to work for what they want?

Materials
- a copy of *Bikes for Rent* by Isaac Olaleye
- a copy of the "Methods of Appeal in Arguments and Propaganda" handout (provided) for each student
- several three-by-three-inch sheets of paper or sticky notes
- a dry-erase or chalk board
- pens and paper for the students

Your students should be familiar with the different methods of creating an argument before you begin this lesson. Spend some time reviewing these techniques, or brainstorm with your students; ask them to list all the methods they use when they try to get something from their parents. When you see that the students understand the different methods of persuasion, proceed with the lesson.

Procedures
1. Read the story to the students, pausing at various points to ask what they think the main character, Lateef, should do during certain situations.

2. At the end of the story, ask the students to take a small piece of paper (or a sticky note) and write down how they think Lateef should resolve his dilemma. The students should *not* write their names on the paper.

3. Have the students fold their papers, and pass around a hat or some other container to collect their responses.

4. Once you have collected all the responses, read them aloud. Facilitate a class discussion in which the students determine whether or not each one is a good solution. Talk about what makes each solution good or bad. Write the "good" responses on the board.

5. Ask the class to vote for the top five, and leave only those responses on the board.

6. Using the five winning responses, have pairs (or groups) of students provide:
   - at least two reasons why the solutions are good ones
   - one example of an emotional, logical, or ethical appeal for the solution

- two possible logical fallacies for each of these solutions (doing this allows students to become more skilled at identifying, and avoiding, logical fallacies in their own arguments)

7. After about thirty minutes, have each group or pair present their reasons and fallacies, and discuss with the class the effectiveness of each presentation. Help the rest of the class determine whether the presenters used an emotional, logical, or ethical appeal to demonstrate why their solutions for Lateef are valid ones. (Consider providing some type of rubric to help the students stay on topic as they evaluate the presentations.) The evaluation of the presentations could function as a type of assessment.

Extensions
- Have students compose an essay in which they argue whether or not children over the age of four should have to work for what they want.
- As a cross-curricular effort, ask the students to research child labor laws and incorporate their findings in the essay.

Methods of Appeal in Arguments and Propaganda

Logical reasoning (LOGOS) One type of logical reasoning applies one or more general principles to reach a conclusion. If the principles are valid, then the conclusion must also be valid. A second type of reasoning draws a general conclusion from a series of examples; if you meet fifty children who like computer games, you might conclude many children like computer games.

Ethical reasoning (ETHOS) The objective is for an audience to believe what the speaker is saying. This is done by establishing trust by finding common ground and establishing credibility. An ethical argument must be objectively stated and should never depend on name-calling.

Emotional reasoning (PATHOS) This method of appeal should never be used on its own. Its main purpose is to make the listener *feel* what is happening. This appeal is most effective when the audience places themselves in the same position. Vivid verbs and engaging anecdotes are critical for creating an effective emotional argument.

Endorsements: Texts and visual representations often attempt to persuade readers by citing authoritative endorsements. For example, an advertisement may claim a product is good and provide ten celebrity endorsements as evidence in an attempt to transfer the trust that people have in the person to the product.

Logical Fallacies: These include half-truths, false analogies, irrelevant information, stating opinions as facts, and oversimplification. The same fallacies found in texts are often also found in media messages. However, remember that not all media messages contain logical fallacies or make exaggerated claims. Many media messages present genuine facts and ideas in an effort to allow viewers to make their own informed judgment.

Glittering Generalities: These are exaggerated claims or statements that are unsupported by facts or ignore exceptions or qualifications.

Lifestyle: Advertisements often use attractive people enjoying a product in an idyllic or peaceful setting in the hope that viewers will transfer the feelings they have about the scene to the product being used. How the people who use the product look is actually irrelevant to how well the product performs.

Bandwagon: The appeal comes from the perception that everyone seems to be using the same tactic or doing the same thing.

Card Stacking: Presenting overwhelming evidence for one side and not the other, or using leading questions that force the consumer to choose the advertised product.

Argumentation

At the end of this lesson, students should be able to identify various methods of appeals within a text as well as create their own.

Earrings! by Judith Viorst

In this book, Judith Viorst humorously allows children to see how creative we can be when it comes to getting something we want. *Earrings!* gives the reader the opportunity to explore argumentative techniques, focusing on the three types of appeals used to create an effective argument.

Materials
- a copy of *Earrings!* by Judith Viorst
- sticky notes
- a copy of the "Methods of Appeal in Arguments and Propaganda" handout (provided in the *Bikes for Rent* lesson) for each student
- a copy of the "Argument Evaluation Chart" handout (provided) for each student

Procedures
1. Give students the handout "Methods of Appeal in Arguments and Propaganda." Review the different types of appeals writers use when creating an argument. You may also want to address different types of propaganda so that students can recognize the types used in *Earrings!*.

2. Read the story aloud to your students, telling them to concentrate on how the little girl tries to convince her parents to give her something they don't want her to have. Students should create a list of the arguments the little girl uses on their "Argument Evaluation Chart."

3. Have the students use the "Methods of Appeal in Arguments and Propaganda" handout to identify the types of arguments (logos, ethos, pathos) and logical fallacies the little girl uses.

4. Have the students defend the labels they assign to each type of argument. This is where they will identify the different strategies the girl uses, thus proving that they understand how a writer would effectively use each type of appeal.

5. As an assessment, have each student or pairs of students submit the different appeals they've identified along with their explanations supporting their identifications.

Extensions
- Have the students pose as the girl's parents and write a response determining whether or not the little girl will get the earrings she so desperately desires. The parents will also have to indicate why they made that particular decision.
- Have the students to write to a parent or another authority figure asking for something they really want. Remind them to use the appeals you've studied in class and avoid logical fallacies.

Argument Evaluation Chart

Argument Presented (What did she say she was going to do?)	Page Number	Strategy Used (Ethos, Logos, Pathos)	Evaluation of the Strategy (Was this a good tactic to use? Why or why not?)

Argumentation

At the end of this lesson, students should be able to properly identify and create various examples of appeals and propaganda.

Ira Sleeps Over by Bernard Waber

A child's first sleepover is one of the most exciting—and terrifying—nights in his or her life. Having a good friend there often helps the night pass more smoothly, but what if that friend is a bear that should have been put away a long time ago? *Ira Sleeps Over* allows teachers to tap into children's recollections of their apprehension about staying away from home for the first time while analyzing methods of persuasion. It also gives students an opportunity to explore the different types of propaganda used in persuasion.

Materials
- a copy of *Ira Sleeps Over* by Bernard Waber
- a copy of the "Methods of Appeal in Arguments and Propaganda" handout (provided in the *Bikes for Rent* lesson) for each student
- several examples of appeals and propaganda from newspapers or magazines

Procedures
1. Read the book up to the line "I decided not to take my teddy bear." Ask the students if they think Ira should take his bear to his first sleepover.

2. As a class, create a large T-chart listing reasons why Ira should or should not take his teddy bear.

3. Divide the students into groups according to the stance they take. Tell the groups to incorporate the different appeals into the reasons on the list. For example, if one reason not to take the bear is that Ira would be teased, the students should create an emotional appeal based on that idea.

4. Allow each group to report and discuss their reasons. The class should evaluate each group's reasoning based on the support provided by the group.

5. After the evaluations, put the students back into smaller groups, and tell them to refer to the "Methods of Appeal in Arguments and Propaganda" handout. Give the students the newspapers and magazines and ask them to find and label different examples of propaganda. Then ask the groups to present their examples and have their classmates determine whether or not the groups accurately identified the different types of propaganda.

6. Assign each group a different type of propaganda, and have them create at least two examples, focusing on deciding whether or not Ira should take his bear.

7. Once the students have completed their propaganda examples, finish reading the story so they know how it all ends. Afterward, ask the students to return to the story and

locate all of the uses of the appeals or propaganda within it. This will give you another opportunity to make a "quick check" assessment to gauge student understanding.

Extensions
- Ask the students to write an essay in favor of or against childhood imaginary friends. Instruct them to use at least two examples of the appeals on the list they created and to include some form(s) of propaganda to show that they understand how it is used in persuasion.
- This lesson serves as a nice introduction to *Julius Caesar* (William Shakespeare) and an examination of how appeals influence argument.

Biography, Making Inferences, and Narrative Structure

At the end of this lesson, students should be able to identify both narrative and biographical writing as well as use text to make and defend inferences.

Grandfather's Journey by Allen Say

In this beautifully illustrated and poignant little book, the narrator introduces us to his grandfather and weaves the story of a man torn between two countries. *Grandfather's Journey* is an excellent resource for introducing biographies and narrative structure.

Materials
- a copy of *Grandfather's Journey* by Allen Say
- craft supplies (markers, construction paper, etc.)
- pens and paper for the students

Procedures
1. Invite the students to think about family stories and legends, the tales that have been told over and over again at family gatherings. The students should make a list of these stories; some will have more than others. Some students may want to include stories about people who are emotionally rather than biologically related to them.

2. Ask the students to think about their favorite family story as you read the book to them.

3. Use the think-aloud strategy to encourage thinking and discussion as you read.
   - Page 7: How do context clues help the reader pinpoint a time period?
   - Page 10: Help students fine tune their ideas about the time period.
   - Page 15: Why would the grandfather return home to find a wife?
   - Page 18: What do the songbirds symbolize?
   - Page 22: Why would the daughter's perspective be different from her parents'?
   - Page 25: Did the symbolism of the songbirds change? Why or why not?
   - Page 26: Which war is being described?
   - Page 28: Why didn't the grandfather get another songbird?
   - Page 31: How is the narrator like his grandfather?
   - Page 32: What does the narrator mean when he says, "I think I know my grandfather now"?

4. Help the students understand how much the narrator shared about his grandfather by recounting just a few biographical events from his life.

5. Encourage the students to select one of their own family stories and turn it into a larger piece. (They may need to talk to other family members to get more details.) Be sure to help students understand and apply the organizational structure of narratives and biographies.

6. Have the students create their own books to tell their stories. They may include photos or other illustrations. Allow for creative latitude.

Extensions
- This would be a great book for introducing literature about the struggles faced by the children of immigrants or even the age-old dilemma of the generation gap. Suggestions include:
  - "The Circuit," a short story by Francisco Jimenez
  - "Everyday Use," a short story by Alice Walker
  - "Two Kinds," a short story by Amy Tan
  - *Cry, the Beloved Country,* a novel by Alan Paton
  - *The House on Mango Street,* a novel by Sandra Cisneros
  - *The Joy Luck Club,* a novel by Amy Tan

Cause and Effect

At the end of this lesson, students should be able to explain how cause and effect are developed in a story.

Thank You, Mr. Falker by Patricia Polacco

This touching (and all-too-true) story allows us to see how one teacher can change the life of a student forever. Through this tale, we are able to carefully examine cause and effect in the situation of a little girl who almost gives up on the joy of education because of a learning difference.

Materials
- a copy of *Thank You, Mr. Falker* by Patricia Polacco (or a set for the entire class)
- several letter-size sheets of paper in two different colors, each one cut into two vertical strips
- several sheets of construction paper
- glue sticks

Procedures
1. Inform the class that they will be exploring the idea that one action can lead to several results. Get students involved by asking them to give situations where this might occur (e.g., not doing your homework can lead to ..., doing your chores around the house can lead to ...).

2. Read the story, instructing the class to listen carefully for all the things that happen to or affect the little girl.

3. After you have finished reading the story, have pairs of students work together to create a two-color, cause-and-effect chart using the sheets of colored paper.

4. Tell the students to glue two different color sheets side by side on a large sheet of construction paper, and label one color "Causes" and the other "Effects."

5. Have the students work together to identify some of the problems described by the author in the story. Then have them list the causes of the problems on the appropriate sheet and the effects on the other.

6. On a separate sheet, have the students talk about each (or a selected number) of causes and effects. They should discuss how those things could have affected the girl or would have affected them if they had been in her situation. The objective is to guide the students in seeing how one action can cause a certain reaction. The examination of cause and effect can also help the students understand the sequencing of events.

Extensions

- Have the students examine the causal relationships listed below as they are relevant to the cause-and-effect essay structure and then produce their own examples of each.
  - **Necessary Cause**: one that must be present for the effect to occur.
    For example: Combustion is necessary for driving a gasoline engine.
  - **Sufficient Cause**: one that can produce an effect unaided, although there may be more than one sufficient cause of a given effect.
    For example: A dead battery can keep a car from starting, but faulty spark plugs or an empty gas tank will have the same effect.
  - **Contributory Cause**: one that helps to produce an effect but cannot do so by itself.
    For example: Running a red light might cause an accident. But other factors— pedestrians or other cars—must also be present.

Characterization

At the end of this lesson, students should be able to create an accurate description of a character in a literary text

Dandelions by Eve Bunting

Young Zoe narrates this tale of her family's covered-wagon journey from Illinois to Nebraska. Her youthful objectivity starkly contrasts and highlights her mother's fears and sadness about the move. The narrator's simple reporting also lends itself easily to a lesson on characterization. Consider teaming up with the history teachers to create an interdisciplinary unit.

Materials
- a copy of *Dandelions* by Eve Bunting
- a copy of the "Character Analysis" chart (provided) for each student
- pens and paper for the students

Procedures
1. As a warm-up, have the students complete a written response to the following questions:
   - Have you ever had to move and leave your friends and family behind?
   - How did you feel?
   - Did you eventually like the new place? If so, how long did it take?
   - Of all that you left behind, what did you miss the most?
   - If you've always lived here, how would you respond if your parents told you tonight that you were moving to another state?

2. Allow the students to share their responses with a classmate who sits near them.

3. Remind the students that in today's society, moving away isn't quite what it was a hundred years ago. Today we have e-mail, webcams, and telephones; people typically move to towns that are full of people, and they can quickly return to what they've left behind via modern transportation. However, for the early settlers of our country, moving often meant long periods of isolation and years between visits to family.

4. Read *Dandelions* (1995 Edition used here), pausing during the following passages to facilitate the students' discussion:
   - page 1, last line: "'But it's so lonely ...,' Mama said." What does this statement most likely foreshadow?
   - page 3, paragraph 2: The author is creating a vivid impression of Mama. What adjective would you use to describe her at this point in the story?
   - page 8, first paragraph: What do you think Mama looked like?
   - page 9, fourth paragraph: Why would it have been a long time since they had seen another woman? Does it seem to matter that the women are apparently of different nationalities? How do we know they are of different nationalities?
   - page 12, second paragraph: Why do you think roses are so important to the women?

- page 14, fourth paragraph: What does this exchange between the children tell us about the two families?
- page 17, last paragraph: What does this conversation tell us about Papa? What does it say about his relationship with Mama?

5. At this point, tell the students that you are going to continue reading without interruption and that they should continue to listen closely for key phrases that develop the plot or the characters.

6. Finish reading the book.

7. Hand out the "Character Analysis" chart. You may wish to have a projection of the chart as you discuss it with students and give them the assignment.

8. Ask the students to fill in the rest of the chart and to support their responses with textual evidence.

9. Review the concept of characterization with the students and facilitate a discussion of Bunting's method of developing her characters. Encourage the students to analyze the methods used by other authors as well.

Extensions
- Ask the students to create character chart for the supporting characters in the story (even the Svensons could be used). This can be done individually or in small groups. Tell the students to support each entry on the chart with passages from the text.
- This is an excellent book for introducing literature about the Westward Movement, such as *My Antonia* (Willa Cather). If doing so, have the students identify the similarities and differences in the characters and the authors' styles.
- Have the students use their warm-up responses to generate a larger memoir of their experience.

Character Analysis: Mama from *Dandelions*

Using the example provided and evidence from the text, complete a character analysis of Mama from *Dandelions*. Place a character trait in each oval, and use the box below the oval to provide textual evidence that supports your description.

Mama

Scared

"See how the grass closes behind us? It's as if we'd never been."

Characterization

At the end of this lesson, students should be able to recognize both direct and indirect characterization within a text and form opinions on how each technique affects a reader's perception of a character.

Wolf by Becky Bloom

When we hear the word "wolf," we don't immediately feel warm and fuzzy. This charming story allows children to see how forming opinions about people (or animals) without getting to know who they truly are can cost them some really good friends. This story serves as the perfect example of characterization—both direct and indirect—by allowing students to clearly see how the author gives readers information about characters as well as guides them toward forming their own opinion about the characters.

Materials
- a copy of *Wolf* by Becky Bloom
- a copy of the "Methods of Characterization" handout (provided) for each student

Make sure that the students understand the basic definitions of indirect and direct characterization.
- Direct Characterization: The author specifically states what kind of person the character is by giving him or her specific personality traits.
  "Cinderella's stepsisters were mean and ugly, and they always treated her unkindly."

- Indirect Characterization: The character is revealed through his or her own actions or words as well as through commentary from other characters.
  "Even though John had always treated Joan with respect, she walked past him and sneered, saying, 'Move, dweeb! No one wants to talk to you!'"

Procedures
1. Read the book aloud, stopping to ask questions that are directly related to characterization:
   - Based on the author's description of the wolf, do you like him? Why or why not?
   - What is your opinion of the other animals he encounters?

(Read the book before the lesson so that you know exactly when to ask these questions and any others you create.)

2. After you have finished reading the book, give the students a chance to discuss the characters—what they liked and disliked.

3. Inform the students that they will lay the groundwork to determine the methods of characterization used by the author.

4. Distribute the "Methods of Characterization" handout, and tell students that they will—individually, in pairs, or in small groups, depending on the chemistry of the classroom—complete a graphic organizer to show the different methods of characterization the author employs.

5. Complete one section with the class to guide their efforts:
   • Indirect Characterization
      i. Instruct the class to find one situation where the character's private thoughts are revealed, for example:
      "The wolf had never been treated like this before. 'Educated animals ... This is something new. Well, then! I'll learn to read too.'"

      ii. Have the students write this information in the correct section of the handout.

6. Inform the students that they will complete the process on their own. (Set a time limit, if you choose.) Remind them that they must support all their observations with evidence from the book.

7. After the students have completed the chart, ask them to consider the following question:
   • Does this character seem to be a stereotype or to represent a specific type of individual? Explain. (This information can be put on the back of the chart and can be used as an opportunity to introduce the concept of satire.)

8. Have each student pair up with a classmate or divide them into groups so they can share their findings. Post the charts around the room so the students can use them as reference points.

If you choose, you can assign certain characters to certain students or groups and have them complete the charts about that one character. After the charts are complete, the students can join others who had the same characters and compare notes, making notations and additions to their own sheets as they see fit.

Extensions
   • This activity can introduce a character analysis essay. It provides students with a solid understanding of how an author creates character types as well as the importance of relevant textual support.
   • Use the second column of the organizer to help students comment on the method of characterization by using phrases such as:
      o "This shows that ..."
      o "Obviously ..."
      o "These actions help the reader to see that ..."
Such commentary can help the students analyze the author's style of writing.

Methods of Characterization

Title of literary piece: _____Student name(s): _____

Author: _____   _____

Methods of Characterization	Textual support and what is revealed about the character
Indirect Characterization	
The author shows what the character does and how the character acts and reacts.	
The author describes what the character looks like and how he or she dresses.	
The author reveals what other characters say or think about the character.	
The character's private thoughts are revealed.	
The character is revealed through his or her own speech.	
Direct Characterization	
The author directly tells the reader what kind of person the character is: funny, mean, snobbish, etc.	

Compare and Contrast

At the end of this lesson, students should be able to utilize the point-by-point and subject-by-subject organizational structures to create their own compare-and-contrast essays.

Sisters by David McPhail

There's nothing like family, the ones we love, the ones we try to love. We all share so many similarities yet we have many differences. David McPhail's story allows readers to examine compare-and-contrast structures, focusing on the shared traits and the distinctions among family members. This lesson allows students to see how authors present characters in different ways.

Materials
- a copy of *Sisters* by David McPhail
- graphic organizer (either a T-chart or another form of organizer)
- a copy of the "Examples of Ways to Organize a Compare/Contrast Essay" handout (provided) for each student

Procedures
1. Tell the students to think about apples and oranges. Create a Venn diagram on the board or a projection device, and ask the students to indicate all the differences and similarities between the two fruits.

2. After students have completed the diagram, distribute the handout and introduce both the point-by-point and subject-by-subject organizational structures for organizing compare/contrast essays. As a class, complete a section of both the point-by-point and subject-by-subject structures (such as Roman numeral II) as it relates to apples and oranges.

3. Next, put the students in small groups of no more than four and have them complete the remaining part of handout. This should take about ten to fifteen minutes. Keep in mind (and remind the students) that these sample organizational structures are simplistic versions of the ones they'll create after they've read the story. Have them post their organizational structures and do a gallery walk, allowing everyone to see what the other groups have done.

4. Bring the students back together, and read *Sisters*, instructing students to pay attention to the similarities and differences between the sisters. You may choose to have the students use another Venn diagram to organize the information as they read. Use this activity to highlight the importance of interacting with text while reading.

5. Once the story is complete, have the students work in pairs to complete an organizational structure, either step-by-step or point-by-point (you may want to assign each type to different groups), using the information they've gathered about each sister while reading the story.

6. As the final assignment, ask the students to compose their own compare-and-contrast essay about the sisters. (You may want to require that they support their observations with textual evidence.)

Extensions
- Have the students compare and contrast a short text (such as a poem or short story) to a larger text (such as a novel) that the class has recently read. Students could do this individually using the organizational structure of their choice, or you may want to divide the class into groups and assign each group either the point-by-point or the subject-by-subject organizational structure.

Example of Ways to Organize a Compare/Contrast Essay

Sports Cars versus SUVs

Subject-by-Subject Organization
Discuss everything about the first subject—all the pros and cons—and then move to the second subject.

I.   Introduction
    a. discuss the differences and similarities between the two

II. Sports Cars
    a. compare first item or area
        i.   commentary
        ii. commentary
    b. compare second item or area
        i.   commentary
        ii. commentary
    c. compare third item or area
        i.   commentary
        ii. commentary

III. SUVs
    a. compare first item or area
        i.   commentary
        ii. commentary
    b. compare second item or area
        i.   commentary
        ii. commentary
    c. compare third item or area
        i.   commentary
        ii. commentary

Point-by-Point Organization
Pick a certain number of items to discuss, such as gas mileage, pricing, and recreational ability. Address each of these items, first as it applies to the sports car, then as it applies to the SUV.

I.   Introduction
    a. discuss the different things you will compare and contrast

II. Gas Mileage
    a. as it relates to the sports car
        i.   example
        ii. example
    b. as it relates to the SUV
        i.   example
        ii. example

III. Pricing
  a. as it relates to the sports car
    i. example
    ii. example
  b. as it relates to the SUV
    i. example
    ii. example

IV. Recreational ability
  a. as it relates to the sports car
    i. example
    ii. example
  b. as it relates to the SUV
    i. example
    ii. example

Creative and Research Writing

At the end of this lesson, students should be able to distinguish between real history and historical fiction and have a better understanding of effective research and documentation.

A. Lincoln and Me by Louise Borden

Children almost never consider the history of one individual—or the time period surrounding his or her existence—as interesting or exciting. Louise Borden's delightful *A. Lincoln and Me* allows readers to explore the life and times of a historical figure. It shows students how any major historical figure can help them learn about other distinguished men and women.

Materials
- a copy of *A. Lincoln and Me* by Louise Borden
- an encyclopedia set or access to a similar type of information
- enough computers for groups of four to use for research, perhaps in the computer lab, if one is available
- pens and paper for the students

Procedures
1. Tell the students that they are going to explore the life of an important historical figure. Read the story, and have the students jot down all the "facts" they believe to be true.

2. Put the students into no more than four groups, and tell them to look at all the "facts" they have written down. Ask them to work together to "dig" for those "facts" in the encyclopedia set and/or computer databases. Their goal is to determine which "facts" are actually true. The students can create a simple chart to assist them in their research. Use these headings for the chart:
   - Suggested "facts" from the story
   - Actual facts
   - Source
   - Complete citation

Extensions
- Have the students research important figures from the past and create their own stories. You can ask them to put all the stories together to form an anthology of historical fiction and include photos and artwork.
- Ask the students to research individuals relevant to a specific time period, possibly related to another topic or literary piece that will be discussed in class.

Descriptive Writing

At the end of this lesson, students should be able to write more vividly and successfully using various methods to put the reader in the scene they are creating.

Dog Breath by Dav Pilkey

This cute story about bad breath will certainly amuse any audience, since we've all been around someone who could use a mint! Students can use this simple tale to employ the idea of "showing" rather than "telling" a story. This lesson allows teachers and students to paint a picture of a scene by using vivid verbs, adjectives, and adverbs.

Materials
- a copy of *Dog Breath* by Dav Pilkey
- several excerpts from the story, already typed on separate sheets of paper (suggestions are provided)

Procedures
1. Read the story to the students, and discuss the simple style of writing the author chose to use (probably to keep the attention of a younger audience).

2. Give pairs (or small groups) of students different excerpts from the story. See the provided suggestions.
   For example: "When the children took Hally Tosis for a walk, everyone else walked on the other side of the street. Even skunks avoided Hally Tosis." (Basically, group together all the sentences from the two side-by-side pages.)

3. Tell the students to rewrite the excerpts and show what happened by adding vivid verbs, adjectives, and adverbs.
   For example: "When the proud children took Hally Tosis, their new best friend, for a walk ..." Remind students that they may need to combine simple sentences to create more developed, sophisticated ones.

4. After the students have rewritten their chunks, have them come back together in a large group. Create a gallery walk all around the room, displaying their newly created sentences.

Extensions
- Find several different copies of "first reader" type books (with several simple sentences), and give one to each of the groups. (If you have several different books, give each student a book to work on as an independent assignment.) The students will be responsible for "showing" what happens in each of the stories by creating more elaborate sentences.

Excerpts from *Dog Breath*

<u>Excerpt One</u> (pages 8–9)

"But the real trouble started … and Hally jumped up to say hello."

<u>Excerpt Two</u> (page 12)

"The next day, Mr. and Mrs. Tosis decided to find a new home for Hally."

<u>Excerpt Three</u> (page 13)

"The children knew that the only way … had a breathtaking view."

<u>Excerpt Four</u> (page 14)

"They hoped that the breathtaking view would take Hally's breath away … but it didn't."

<u>Excerpt Five</u> (page 28)

"The next morning, the Tosis family awoke to find two burglars passed out cold on their living room floor."

Descriptive Writing

At the end of the lesson, students should be able to write descriptive details to help the reader "see" the picture they are attempting to paint.

Lincoln: A Photobiography by Russell Freedman

Russell Freedman's book shows students that great stories aren't always told with words. Many times, pictures say just as much, if not more. This book is perfect for helping students interpret visuals and use their own imaginations to tell a detailed story, which is imperative for descriptive writing.

Materials
* a copy of *Lincoln: A Photobiography* by Russell Freedman
* photocopies of photos from the book, enough for at least five groups of students (scan each of the pictures and then print them out separately so that students can manipulate them easily; if you are not able to print that many photos, create a power point and label the pictures)

Procedures
1. Tell the students to pay close attention as you read this book about Abraham Lincoln to them because afterward you'll ask them to match pictures with sentences.

2. Read the text aloud, stopping occasionally to ask questions.

   Sample Excerpt
   "Abraham Lincoln wasn't the sort of man who could lose himself in a crowd. After all, he stood six feet, four inches tall, and, to top it off, he wore a silk hat. His height was mostly in his long, bony legs. When he sat in a chair, he seemed no taller than anyone else. It was only when he stood up that he towered above others."

   Sample Question
   What might a picture illustrating this passage look like?

3. Explain that artists get clues on what to draw from the text.

4. Continue reading the book, using this process two to three more times to get the students used to the idea of generating pictures from the sentences in the text.

5. Put the students in small groups of no more than four. Give them pre-selected passages from the book and include certain photos.

6. Instruct the students to take turns reading the passages. Afterward, they should look at the photos and decide as a group which photos go with which passages.

7. Move through the class listening as the groups read and share. Facilitate higher-level questioning; ask the students to be prepared to justify (in writing) why they think a particular photo goes with a sentence group.

8. Have the groups present their findings to the class; the students should determine whether or not they agree with the combinations of photos and text.

9. Place all the photos in a central location where everyone has access, and have the students (individually or in pairs, depending on how many photos are available) select a photo and write a one-page description of it. You may want to include specific parameters, such as "be sure to discuss what he was thinking or the possible conflict in the scene."

10. Base your assessment on the final product of the one page essay, which the students will turn in to you along with the original picture. We recommend creating a rubric with the class so that they know exactly what you are looking for in the final paper.

Extensions
- Since this is about Abraham Lincoln, consider having the students complete a research piece that includes other pictures they can find related to Lincoln or the time period.
- This lesson easily could be adapted for any major figure in history. As a cross-curricular piece, ask the students to conduct a biographical study of a historical figure they are studying in another class.

Dialect

At the end of this lesson, students should be able to analyze how and why authors use language registers and regional dialect.

Raising Sweetness by Diane Stanley

This adorable tale allows children to see how phrases can have different meanings, depending on where a person is from. It allows the teacher to focus on how authors use certain phrases to represent specific time periods or portray specific messages.

Materials
- a copy of *Raising Sweetness* by Diane Stanley
- resource of your choice for reviewing/teaching the five language registers (one can easily be found online)
- pens and paper for the students

Procedures
1. Review the five language registers with students. Have students create their own examples for each register to demonstrate that they can apply their understanding of language registers.

2. Read the book to the students, and instruct them make a list of any words and phrases they hear but don't understand.

3. When you have finished the book, ask the class if they understood everything the author was trying to say. Allow a short discussion of their responses.

4. Put the class into small groups or pairs, and assign each group a number. Have them review all the words and phrases they listed, and tell them to try to translate them into a more modern meaning.

5. Read the story again, but this time inform the students that they should stand up when you call their number and give their translation of the word or phrase mentioned at that point. Ask the rest of the class to evaluate their translation. (Don't tell them if they are correct yet!)

6. Afterward, have the students write a short paragraph explaining the real message of the book. This will allow you to determine if the students really understand the underlying message and theme of the book.

Extensions
- This lesson can be used to introduce students to more difficult texts, such as *The Adventures of Huckleberry Finn* (Mark Twain) or *Their Eyes Were Watching God* (Zora Neale Hurston), which have challenging dialect. It helps students to see that sometimes it is necessary to add colorful phrases to writing to adequately portray the characters or setting.
- Give students various excerpts with challenging dialect from a text you are about to begin (such as a Shakespeare piece), and have them recreate the passage using modern phrasing.

Diction

At the end of this lesson, students should be able to explore effective word selection, or diction, with the understanding that changing certain words can make a big difference in how the text is received.

Miss Nelson Is Missing by James Marshall

At one time or another, every student wishes he or she had a different teacher … until they get a teacher that makes them realize just how good they really had it. Sometimes students don't realize that certain words can have a big impact on how people interpret and receive information.

Materials
- a copy of *Miss Nelson Is Missing* by James Marshall
- strips of paper with teacher-selected sentences from the book
- a dry-erase board or chalk board
- pens and paper for the students

Procedures
1. Inform the students that the lesson will concentrate on diction; as they listen to the story, they should write down phrases that stand out.

2. Read the story. Ask the students to tell you which phrases stand out to them and why. (Write or place some of those phrases on the board.) Discuss how diction helps the reader identify and understand the author's tone and how he or she chose to portray information.

3. Distribute the sentences you selected from the text, and have the students rewrite the sentences using different words to create a stronger or weaker feeling.

    Example:
      Original text: "Now settle down."
      Revision: "Sit down, and shut up right now!"

4. Put the students in pairs or small groups, and give each group one or two of the sentences from the text. Ask each group to write a sentence that creates the opposite feeling of the original.

5. Have them place a few of their new sentences on the board. Talk about why the author chose the original sentences and what that says about the character who is speaking.

Extensions
- Have each student pick a partner; direct both to write a descriptive paragraph (on any subject of their choice), one positive, the other negative. Then have students create one more paragraph—this time, together—about the same topic but using neutral diction.

Extended Metaphor

At the end of this lesson, students should be able to identify an extended metaphor and use text to describe and defend the metaphor.

Mrs. Spitzer's Garden by Edith Pattou

Mrs. Spitzer is an avid gardener who delights in planting seeds and growing things. At first glance, it seems as though she has a regular garden; however, the reader comes to realize that Mrs. Spitzer is a teacher who is nurturing her students. *Mrs. Spitzer's Garden* is an excellent tool for teaching about the extended metaphor. It isn't until the book is almost completed that readers realize this is no ordinary garden.

Materials
- a copy of *Mrs. Spitzer's Garden* by Edith Pattou
- a copy of the "No Ordinary Garden" handout (provided) for each student
- pens and paper for the students

Procedures
1. Read the book to the students, allowing them to discover the metaphor for themselves.

2. When you are finished, ask the students to write a short response to the book, highlighting anything they found special or interesting.

3. Ask the students to share what they've written with a classmate who sits near them.

4. Allow a few volunteers to share their written responses with the whole class.

5. Reveal the concept of the extended metaphor.

6. Have the students complete the "No Ordinary Garden" handout to identify the ways the author compares young people to plants in a garden.

7. Facilitate a class discussion about why an author might use an extended metaphor and the resulting impact on the reader.

Extensions
- Have the students generate a list of common events in their lives (e.g., homework, school, chores, etc.). Then ask them to complete the following statement for each event:

  _____ is like _____ because _____.

  Example:
  Homework is like *dust* because *there's always more of it*.

Tell the students to choose their favorite sentence, and use it to create a piece (poetry or prose) that incorporates an extended metaphor.

- Read a larger piece that utilizes an extended metaphor. Suggestions include:
  - *Guessing Game,* a short story by Rose Million Healey
  - *Animal Farm*, a novel by George Orwell
  - *Dracula*, a novel by Bram Stoker
  - *The Great Gatsby,* a novel by F. Scott Fitzgerald

No Ordinary Garden

In each circle branching from the center, identify an action that Mrs. Spitzer takes to care for her garden. In the box beneath each circle, describe what that action might look like in a classroom rather than in a garden. The first one is done for you as an example.

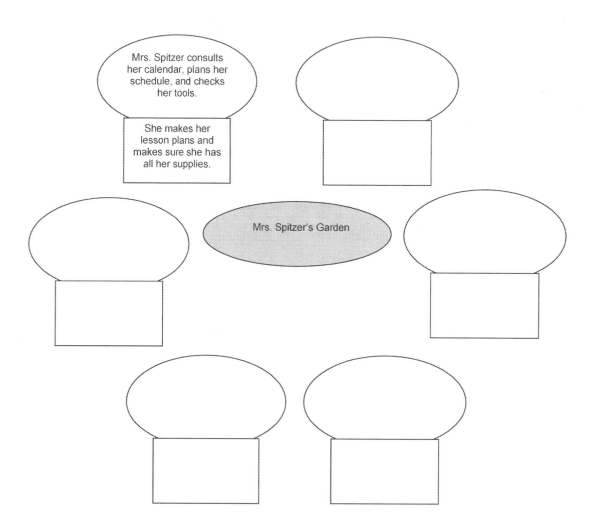

Mrs. Spitzer consults her calendar, plans her schedule, and checks her tools.

She makes her lesson plans and makes sure she has all her supplies.

Mrs. Spitzer's Garden

Folklore

At the end of this lesson, students should be able to identify forms of folklore and have an awareness of folklore from a variety of cultures.

Grandmother's Dreamcatcher by Becky Ray McCain

Grandmother's Dreamcatcher is a wonderfully illustrated book that describes the history and importance of the dreamcatcher, a Native American tradition. As an added bonus, the author includes directions for making a traditional dreamcatcher. This book has many uses for the classroom. It is an excellent tool for exploring the genre of folklore as well as for introducing a multicultural unit to encourage students to share traditions and beliefs unique to their cultures.

Materials
* a copy of *Grandmother's Dreamcatcher* by Becky Ray McCain
* pens and paper for the students

Procedures
1. As a warm-up, have the students complete a written response to the following prompt: Write about a tradition or story that is important to your family.

2. Allow the students to share their responses with a partner, and then ask a few volunteers to share with the whole class.

3. Tell the students that you're going to share a tradition from another culture with them.

4. Read *Grandmother's Dreamcatcher*.

5. Ask the students to take two minutes to respond in writing. Tell them to write about what the book made them think and feel.

6. Again, allow the students to share their written responses with a partner, and then ask a few volunteers to share with the whole class.

7. Tell the students that many families have cultural and familial beliefs and stories that they pass orally from generation to generation.

8. Inform the students that literature includes a genre that incorporates this oral tradition. It's called folklore, and it includes the following kinds of stories:
   * tall tale
   * myth
   * legend
   * ghost stories

9. Divide the students into groups, and assign each group one of the four folklore categories listed above. As most classes have more than twelve to sixteen students, consider the following options:
   - Allow more than one group to do each topic.
   - Allow one group to research the genre of folklore, its origins, etc.
   - Include urban legends as a category.
   - Assign specific cultures, such as Native American folklore, Asian folklore, etc., to a few groups.

10. Each group should create a presentation that includes the following components:
    - definition of the category
    - origin (if known)
    - examples

11. It is your choice whether the students use poster board, PowerPoint, or another presentation tool. Allow students to help you make the rubric by which the presentations will be graded.

Extensions
   - Invite a guest speaker (or several) to share culturally specific folklore with the class. Your students can help you identify and invite the speakers.
   - Use *Grandmother's Dreamcatcher* to introduce a longer example of Native American literature, such as *The Last of the Mohicans* (James Fenimore Cooper).
   - Ask the students to write their own folktales, perhaps using their own family traditions or stories.

Historical Context

At the end of this lesson, students should be able to evaluate the effects of war on the characters and understand how historical context affects literature.

Pink and Say by Patricia Polacco

Characteristic of Polacco's style, this tale tugs at the heartstrings. It brings the Civil War to life through the experiences of two young men caught on opposite sides. *Pink and Say* is the perfect book for introducing any larger literary piece that has war at the center of its plot. It objectively points out the human side of war.

Materials
- a copy of *Pink and Say* by Patricia Polacco
- American war timeline (one can easily be found online)
- pens and paper for the students

Procedures
1. Facilitate a class discussion on the topic of war and America's role in conflict. As students sometimes arrive in a classroom with limited knowledge, use the timeline to remind or inform them how many wars America has fought. Remember that this topic often provokes strong feelings; ask students to be objective, choose their words carefully, and avoid blanket generalizations.

2. Because Polacco uses language from the time period, there may be words your students do not know. You may want to have the students complete a vocabulary lesson using those words or simply post the words and their definitions as you read. Words that may be troublesome include:
   - lad
   - mahogany
   - "go green" (gangrene)
   - marauders
   - tote (verb)
   - vittles
   - "jumped the broom" (got married)
   - root cellar
   - buckboard
   - smote
   - hemp

3. Read *Pink and Say*.

4. Have the students generate a short written response that focuses on their reactions to the text. Allow volunteers to share their responses.

5. Ask students to choose one of the following quotes from Moe Moe Bay and write what it means to them.
   - "Child, bein' brave don't mean you ain't afeared."
   - "They's things worse than death, child."

6. Introduce the literary work that the class will be studying (some suggestions listed below), and ask the students to think about the day's discussion and their written responses while they read. Their goal is to make connections throughout the study.
    *   *A Separate Peace,* by John Knowles
    *   *All Quiet on the Western Front,* by Erich Maria Remarque
    *   *Fallen Angels,* by Walter Dean Myers
    *   *The Things They Carried,* by Tim O'Brien

Extensions
*   Team up with the history teacher to put together an interdisciplinary unit that incorporates the literary work your class is studying.
*   Invite veterans to come talk to your class about their experiences. (Your students and colleagues can help you find willing speakers, as can your local chapter of the Veterans of Foreign Wars.) Record the presentation so that other classes can see it as well.
*   Return to the American war timeline. Divide the students into groups, and assign a different war to each one. Have the groups create three-to-five minute factual presentations about their assigned wars. In this way, the students can gain greater knowledge about the wars fought by the United States.

Historical Context

At the end of this lesson, students should be able to list several key facts about the Great Depression and use text to identify and defend the historical context in a literary work.

Potato: A Tale from the Great Depression by Kate Lied

This delightfully illustrated book follows one family's struggle to survive the Great Depression. *Potato* is a great tool for introducing the importance of historical context or biographical and narrative writing. It can also be used as a springboard to larger literary works set during the Depression.

Materials
- multiple copies of *Potato: A Tale from the Great Depression* by Kate Lied
- a strategy for creating flexible groups, such as these food category signs. Print each of the following categories of food on separate sheets of paper and hang them in different areas of the room.
    - Chinese food (fried rice, egg rolls, etc.)
    - desserts (cake, cookies, etc.)
    - fast food (burgers, fries, chicken nuggets, etc.)
    - Italian food (pizza, spaghetti, etc.)
    - Mexican food (tacos, enchiladas, etc.)
    - Southern food (chicken-fried steak, fried chicken, etc.)
    - vegetarian food (soy products, tofu, etc.)
- large pieces of paper (butcher paper or flip-chart paper)
- markers
- pens and paper for the students

Procedure
1. As a warm-up, ask students to get with a partner and answer the following questions: What is your favorite food? Why do you like it so much? Do you remember the first time you ever had it?

2. Draw students' attention to the signs you have posted around the room that indicate different categories of food. Ask the students to stand next to the sign that best matches their favorite food. If you have students whose favorite foods do not fit into any of those categories, allow them to become their own group. If any group appears too large, split it into two.

3. Within their groups, give the students enough time (three to five minutes) to share their responses to the warm-up exercise with each other.

4. While the students are sharing, give each group a large piece of paper and a marker. Make sure that each group has a different color of marker.

5. Tell each group to use the paper and marker to list the things they know about the Great Depression. Lessen their anxiety by reminding them that it is okay if their current knowledge of the topic is limited.

6. After the groups have finished their lists, allow them to walk around the room to look at the other lists. They should take their markers with them. Have students use their markers to add anything that they know about the Great Depression that is not already on another group's list.

7. Once each group has returned to its own list, tell the students to sit down.

8. Give each group a copy of *Potato* and have them read it. They can either choose a reader or take turns.

9. When each group is finished, have them compile a list of quotes from the book that provide facts about the time period and thereby establish the historical context.

10. Tell the group that finishes first to write their quotes on the board. As other groups finish, have them add anything they found that is not already listed on the board.

11. Lead a discussion to evaluate the information on the board and ensure that all of the posted quotes add to the historical context of the book.

12. Finally, facilitate a discussion with the students about *why* the historical context of a book matters. How does it influence what the characters do and say?

Extensions
- Have students complete a research project that focuses on the Great Depression.
- Use this lesson to introduce a larger literary piece that is set in the Great Depression, such as *The Grapes of Wrath* or *Of Mice and Men* (John Steinbeck).

Idioms and Words with Multiple Meanings

At the end of this lesson, students should be able to explain what an idiom is and know how to use several common idioms.

A Chocolate Moose for Dinner by Fred Gwynne

To the ears of our young narrator, the things people say don't make much sense. After all, why would you eat a chocolate moose for dinner? This book does an excellent job of exploring the world of idioms and words with multiple meanings. It also highlights the importance of background knowledge.

Materials
- a copy of *A Chocolate Moose for Dinner* by Fred Gwynne
- "Why Is the English Language So Hard to Learn?" document (provided) projected on a screen or posted on the classroom wall
- a list of common idioms (one can easily be found online)
- large index cards

Procedures
1. Ask the students if they've ever tried to learn a foreign language.

2. Ask the students if they think English is an easy language to learn.

3. Display the document "Why Is the English Language So Hard to Learn?"

4. Invite the students to share their thoughts about using words with more than one meaning.

5. Explain that the English language can be difficult because it uses many idioms and words with multiple meanings.

6. Show the students the definition of idiom.

7. Give students the list of common idioms, and ask the students to explain each one. Share the actual meanings, if they get them wrong.

8. Read *A Chocolate Moose for Dinner* to the class. Discuss the idioms and words with multiple meanings used in the text.

9. Distribute the index cards.

10. Ask the students to create cards for two "newer" idioms that they use and think people should know. You may want to use this template:

Idiom	Meaning of the idiom
Visual depiction of what the idiom means	Visual depiction of what the idiom does not mean

Extensions
- Ask the students to select a common idiom and research its background in a short, documented essay.
- Ask students to conduct a scavenger hunt for idioms in their reading. Consider giving the students extra credit for the idioms they find.

Why Is the English Language So Hard to Learn?

The bandage was wound around the wound.

The farm was used to produce produce.

The dump was so full that it had to refuse more refuse.

He could lead if he would get the lead out.

The soldier decided to desert his dessert in the desert.

Since there is no time like the present, he thought it was time to present the present.

I did not object to the object.

There was a row among the oarsmen about how to row.

They were too close to the door to close it.

To help with planting, the farmer taught his sow to sow.

The wind was too strong to wind the sail.

Upon seeing the tear in the painting, I shed a tear.

I had to subject the subject to a series of tests.

Imagery

At the end of this lesson, students should be able to write vivid descriptions using effective adjectives and elaboration techniques.

The Night I Followed the Dog by Nina Laden

This book allows students to see how words create vivid pictures for the reader, which makes it ideal for teaching about imagery. Students can also discover the importance of descriptive adjectives and identifying nouns within a text.

Materials
- a copy of *The Night I Followed the Dog* by Nina Laden
- several sticky notes for each group or pair of students
- several short passages from any text the class is reading, with the adjectives removed

Procedures
1. Read the story aloud to your students, telling them to write down the words that have been "drawn" for the reader.

   Sample Question
   The word "limousine" is drawn as a car rather than written as a word. What words would you use to describe the vehicle?

2. After you finish reading the story, ask students to go back and look at each of the words they have selected or noticed. Tell them to use sticky notes to indicate the adjectives they would use to create a better "picture" of those words.

3. Put students in small groups of no more than four. Have them share with the group the words they chose to describe, and select the best three examples from the group to present to the class.

4. Have the groups present their findings to the class, encouraging discussion on the most descriptive words.

5. Give students the passages you chose and from which you have removed the adjectives. Have each student create his or her own adjectives for the nouns in the excerpt. This forces the students to consider the appropriate descriptive words as well as concentrate on the nouns themselves.

Extensions
- Have the students create a story about a topic of your choice. Tell them to use a prescribed number of adjectives to help the reader get a clear picture of the nouns being presented. You may want to provide story starter sentences to help the students get started.

Irony

At the end of this lesson, students should be able to identify irony within a text, determine the meaning behind the irony, and discuss what effect that device has on the text.

Cinderella

The classic story of Cinderella is familiar to many students, but most never take the time to "discover" the literary devices in the text. This moralistic tale about treating others fairly is an excellent example of irony. Several of the characters find themselves in situations they never anticipated, and students are given the opportunity to explore the effects of the ironic situations woven throughout the text.

Materials
- a copy of *Cinderella* (several different versions are available, but the children's story is best for this lesson)
- a PowerPoint version of the story if available (optional)
- a dry-erase board or chalk board
- several large (such as eleven-by-seventeen-inch) sheets of construction paper

Procedures
1. Prior to reading the story, make sure that the students know the three major types of irony that exist in literature. Ask them to give examples after you explain each type.
   - Situational irony: a contrast between what is intended or expected and what actually occurs
   - Verbal irony: a figure of speech in which there is a contrast between what is said and what is actually meant
   - Dramatic irony: when the audience knows something that is pertinent to a particular character but the character does not

2. Once it is clear that the students understand the different types of irony, read the book to the class.

3. Have students get in small groups of no more than four and create the chart below on a large sheet of construction paper.

Type of Irony	Where it is found (page #)	How it affects the text (commentary)
Verbal		
Situational		
Dramatic		

4. Give the groups ten to fifteen minutes to complete the chart with examples of irony from the story. If you have a PowerPoint version of the story available, loop the slides so that the students have a chance to refer back to specific situations in the text.

5. The groups should then exchange charts and determine whether their classmates' examples of irony and explanations of how the irony affects the text are correct. The teacher should actively monitor the groups during this process, offering assistance when needed.

Extensions
- Have the students find other examples of Cinderella (Perrault, Grimm, etc.) and create an additional chart with several examples of irony that were found in the story.

Letter Writing

At the end of this lesson, students should know the parts of formal and casual letters and be able to effectively compose either type of letter.

Click, Clack, Moo: Cows That Type by Doreen Cronin

Many students experience difficulty when writing correspondence, as they are often unsure about when a letter should be casual or formal. Students will enjoy this lesson, which gives them specific examples of letters that have been sent to real corporations. *Click, Clack, Moo* allows students to see the basics of letter writing and teachers to present the correct way to create both personal and professional letters.

Materials
- copies of three books:
  - *Click, Clack, Moo: Cows that Type* by Doreen Cronin
  - *Unwritten Letters* by Ilene Segalove
  - *Letters from a Nut* by Ted L. Nancy and Jerry Seinfeld
- several sheets of casual stationery paper (for personal letters) and one box of formal business stationery paper (for professional letters), both of which can be purchased at any local dollar store (typing paper can be substituted for the professional stationery, although it is important for students to be able to see and feel the difference between the two types)
- envelopes
- several examples of both formal and personal letters; many can be found in *Letters from a Nut*
- a dry-erase board and markers or a projection device
- several copies of letters that appear in *Click, Clack, Moo: Cows That Type*; make sure these letters are labeled (i.e., letter A, letter B, etc.)

Procedures
1. Read the story, showing the pictures as you go.

2. Inform the students that they are about to begin or review letter writing. Ask them to name the major parts of a letter. Put their responses on the board. Correct any errors they may make.

3. Ask them how an envelope should be labeled. Draw an envelope on the board, and label those parts as well.

4. Show the students samples of formal and informal letters, and point out the parts they missed. Several examples can be found in any grammar or writing textbook.

5. Read a few examples from *Letters from a Nut*, and ask the class how the authors "sound" in their letters. Do they sound reputable, silly, serious, demented, etc.? Discuss their reasons for assigning these traits.

6. Place the students into pairs or groups of no more than three. Only four letters appear *Click, Clack, Moo*; assign a different one to each group. Ask students in groups one to four to look at their letter, and use it to create a formal letter. Tell group five to write a personal letter from a farmer telling a friend what is happening on the farm. Group six (if needed) can pretend to be a cow writing to tell all of the other farm animals how they can get what they want. Let the students decide for themselves whether they should use formal or personal stationery, given the nature of the letter. If applicable, students should create a name and address for their company and put it on "letterhead" similar to the examples you have provided. Allow approximately twenty to thirty minutes for this activity.

7. The groups should turn in their letters in properly addressed envelopes. Evaluate their work based on proper formatting, completed parts, and presentation.

Extensions
- Using *Unwritten Letters*, provide the students with several ways to start a letter and ask them to complete a letter and address an envelope.
- Ask the students to identify something they would like to receive from or criticize about a large corporation (such as Nike, Polo, Chevron, etc.). Have them research how to contact the company. Suggest that they actually send in a letter and wait for a response.

Literary Devices

At the end of this lesson, students should be able to recognize and analyze a variety of literary devices.

Switch on the Night by Ray Bradbury

Students may be surprised to learn that science fiction writer Ray Bradbury also wrote a beautiful children's book. This wonderfully illustrated book is perfect for teaching literary devices, such as alliteration, personification, and repetition. What a great way to teach literary devices and introduce a longer Bradbury piece!

Materials
- several copies of *Switch on the Night* by Ray Bradbury
- poster paper and markers
- pens and paper for the students

Procedures
1. As a warm-up, have the students complete a written response to the following prompt: When you were younger, were you afraid of the dark? Why? Can you explain your fear? Or, if you weren't afraid, explain why.

2. Invite volunteers to share their responses. As most children go through a stage of being afraid of the dark, this topic will likely spark a lively discussion and give your students an opportunity to find things in common with their peers.

3. Let the students know that the story you will share with them is about a young boy who is afraid of the dark. Tell them that as they listen to the story, they should pay special attention to the literary devices Bradbury uses.

4. Read *Switch on the Night*.

5. Divide students into small groups, and assign each group one of the following literary devices (it is okay if you do not have enough groups to assign them all):
   - alliteration
   - irony
   - personification
   - point of view
   - repetition
   - simile
   - symbolism
   - theme

6. Tell the groups to use a copy of the book to find textual examples of the literary device they have been assigned.

7. Provide the groups with a large piece of paper and markers, and ask them to create a poster that explains their literary device and the examples they've found in the text.

8. Allow each group to share its poster with the whole class.

Extensions
- Use this tale to introduce a longer Bradbury piece, such as the short stories "A Sound of Thunder" or "The Pedestrian" or the novels *Dandelion Wine* or *Fahrenheit 451*.
- Ask the students to brainstorm about other opposites that could be represented in the same way "light" and "night" are in this tale, and generate a poem to showcase their new perspective.

Literary Devices

At the end of this lesson, students should be able to recognize and describe a variety of literary devices, including anaphora, foreshadowing, and symbolism.

The Yellow Star: The Legend of King Christian X of Denmark by Carmen Agra Deedy

This beautifully illustrated book highlights the legend of a Danish king who supported the plight of Danish Jews suffering under the Nazi regime. The author masterfully uses a variety of literary devices, making the book an excellent teaching tool. It would also make a wonderful introduction to a longer piece about the Holocaust.

Materials
- a copy of The Yellow Star: The Legend of King Christian X of Denmark by Carmen Agra Deedy
- a teaching tool of your choice (projection, handout, etc.) for the following literary devices:
  - anaphora
  - dialogue
  - foreshadowing
  - personification
  - repetition
  - simile
  - symbolism
  - theme
- pens and paper for the students

Procedures
1. Read the story to the students without introducing it or giving them an assignment.

2. Review the literary elements listed above using the teaching tool of your choice.

3. Read the story again, this time asking the students to note when they hear one of the discussed literary devices used in the text.

4. Allow the students to share their findings with a partner or in small groups of three or four.

5. Select a scribe to come forward and write a list of the devices found by the students. Let the student sharing each device support his claim with an example from the book. Tell the scribe to list both the device and the example on the board.

6. Have the students complete or add to their notes; ensure that they have identified all of the targeted devices as well as a definition and an example of each.

Extensions

- This book is a nice introduction to literature about the Holocaust, such as:
  - *Night*, by Elie Wiesel
  - *No News from Auschwitz*, by A. M. Rosenthal
  - *Number the Stars*, by Lois Lowry
  - *The Diary of a Young Girl*, by Anne Frank
- Challenge the students to write a one-page story that features three or more of the studied devices. You may want to provide a few story starters to facilitate this activity. Students can also complete this activity in small groups.
- Ask the students to find examples of these devices in other texts (especially if you use this book to introduce longer pieces); consider giving extra credit for every example they find.

Literary Devices and Author's Purpose

At the end of this lesson, students should be able not only to identify certain literary devices but also to create their own questions to ensure a better understanding of the text and the author's purpose.

Thank You, Mr. Falker by Patricia Polacco

A learning disability can turn a child's excitement about school into a nightmare. This is the true story of a special teacher who helps a young girl see past the ugly exterior she sees when she looks at herself. This text allows students to focus on several literary devices and examine the author's purpose.

Materials
- several copies of *Thank You, Mr. Falker* by Patricia Polacco
- a copy of the "Common Literary Devices" handout (provided) for each student (these could be printed two to a page to save paper)
- a copy of Bloom's Taxonomy Question Stems (one can easily be found online) for each student

Procedures
1. Give the students the "Common Literary Devices" handout; make sure they are familiar with the devices and how they look or function in literature.

2. Read the story to the students, asking them to note any literary devices they recognize in the text. You may want to ask probing questions like:
    - What effect does this literary device have on the story?
    - Why would the author have chosen this literary device for this part of the story or sentence?
    - Is there a specific reason why you think the author might have used one type of device in this sentence rather than another type?

3. After you have finished reading the story, give students the handout of Bloom's Taxonomy. Take some time to discuss the different levels of the taxonomy and the fact that the higher levels promote higher thinking skills. Have them work in groups to create questions related to the book that use question stems from all levels of Bloom's Taxonomy. Their questions may be general at this point.

4. If possible, give a copy of the book to each group. Have them create two questions from each level of Bloom's Taxonomy about the author's use of literary devices, citing specific incidents from the text that reflect those devices.

5. Collect all of the student-created questions; then make a mock quiz, and have the students complete and grade the quiz in class.

6. Allow the students to discuss the quiz and decide whether the questions were written effectively. Encourage the students to explore how each question helped expand their

understanding of the story (e.g., "The question regarding the young girl's personality change after working with the teacher helped me to focus on character types").

7. Using the book, encourage students to have a more in-depth discussion of all the devices that were previously identified.

8. Once you feel the students have a better understanding of the story, give them an opportunity to create another set of questions. Have one group pose its questions to another group. (The goal is for the students to create better, more in-depth questions that will lead to deeper discussion among their classmates.)

Extensions
- Using any text the class is reading, have each student create one question from each level of Bloom's Taxonomy, and place all the questions in a container. Instruct students to sit in a circle, and pass the container around. Each student should pull a question out of the container and respond to it. Other students can discuss the question or their peer's response if they choose. This is the beginning stage of Socratic questioning.

Common Literary Devices

- allusion
- archetype
- character
- conflict
- diction
- figure of speech
- flashback
- foreshadowing
- Freytag's pyramid
- hyperbole
- imagery
- irony
- metaphor
- mood
- oxymoron
- paradox
- personification
- plot
- point of view
- pun
- satire
- setting
- simile
- suspense
- symbolism
- syntax
- theme
- tone

Sound Devices

- alliteration
- assonance
- consonance
- onomatopoeia
- rhyme

Logic and Logical Fallacy

At the end of this lesson, students should be able to evaluate a statement for logic and use their knowledge to craft a piece of persuasive writing.

Which Would You Rather Be? by William Steig

This adorable book poses what appear to be very simple questions. However, a little extra thought proves that these simple questions can have complex answers. Many students struggle with logical thinking and recognizing logical fallacies. *Which Would You Rather Be?* helps encourage them to make choices based on sound logic.

Materials
- a copy of *Which Would You Rather Be?* by William Steig
- pens and paper for the students

Procedures
1. As a warm-up, ask the students to list all the choices they have made that day, such as:
    - choosing to attend school
    - choosing what to wear
    - choosing what to have for breakfast (and possibly lunch)
    - choosing how to behave appropriately in class

2. Facilitate a short class discussion about choices. Ask the students if they feel as though they have many choices at this point in their lives. Why or why not? How do they feel about that?

3. Let students know that they are about to make a very serious choice.

4. Read *Which Would You Rather Be?* all the way through one time.

5. Ask the students to listen as you read the book a second time and to choose one of the options described. For example, if the choice is to be a stick or a stone, they should pick one and write that choice on their paper using the following format (you may want to write this on the board):

    I choose to be a _____ rather than a _____.

6. Read the book a second time, pausing briefly after each option so the students can write their choice statements.

7. Have the students turn their choice statements into paragraphs that defend their decisions. If your students need additional structure, tell them that they need a specific number of reasons to support their choices.

8. Ask the students to take their paragraphs and find a partner. (Or assign a partner to each student.)

9. Tell the students to read their paragraphs aloud to their partners. The partners should listen closely to ensure that all of the reader's reasons are logical. As an example, share the following with the students:

"One of the choices presented was to be a grown-up or a kid. Many of you may think that being a grown-up is better because grown-ups can do whatever they want. This is faulty logic. It is not true that grown-ups can do whatever they want. They must find a means of supporting themselves, they cannot break the law without consequences, and they cannot live selfishly if they are in a marital or parental relationship."

10. After each partnership finishes sharing their paragraphs, give them time to revise any identified areas of faulty logic.

11. Have the students develop their paragraphs into larger pieces of persuasive writing in which they set out to prove that they have made the best choice.

Extensions
- Allow the students to share their essays with the class, particularly if two students took opposite sides on the same topic.
- Use this lesson to introduce a unit on logical fallacy and persuasive techniques.
- Have students find and bring in examples of faulty logic in the media or television programs.

Making Inferences and Drawing Conclusions

At the end of this lesson, students should be able to use context clues to make inferences and draw conclusions.

The Gardener by Sarah Stewart

This delightful book chronicles the correspondence between Lydia Grace and her family as they struggle during the Great Depression. *The Gardener* is a gem for teaching students to make inferences and draw conclusions.

Materials
- a copy of *The Gardener* by Sarah Stewart
- pens and paper for the students

Procedures
1. Before you start to read, inform the students that they should adopt the persona of detectives. Tell them to try to "read between the lines" to determine the underlying conflict in the story.

2. Tell students that, as you read, they should take informal notes of the clues they gather from the text and the illustrations. They should focus on setting, characterization, and facts.

3. When you have finished reading the book, allow the students to compare notes with a partner. Each partnership will be responsible for reporting what they believe to be relevant clues and inferences for determining what the book is about.

4. Select a scribe to go to the board, and make a list of clues and inferences as each partnership shares one or two thoughts.

5. When everyone's clues and inferences have been listed, ask the class to come to consensus on the underlying conflict of the story, which is the hardship experienced by a family during the Great Depression.

6. Lead a class discussion about why an author would create a story in the manner used by Stewart.

7. Have the students write a narrative that uses subtlety to reveal the story. It could be a real event from their lives, a perspective on a historical event, or completely fictional. Other books that could be used as models include:
   - *Regarding the Fountain,* by Kate Klise
   - *The Griffin & Sabine Trilogy,* by Nick Bantock

Extensions
- Have the class select a time period or important historical event. Then, have the students write a research-based narrative relevant to that topic. Bind the individual narratives into a book that will become a reference tool related to the time period or event.

Making Inferences and Reading Comprehension

At the end of this lesson, students should be able to articulate what they are thinking while they read and use the text to make and defend inferences.

Dear Mrs. LaRue: Letters from Obedience School by Mark Teague

Join Ike the dog in obedience school. Through the dog's correspondence to his owner, Mrs. LaRue, the reader learns that Ike just might be exactly where he belongs. *Dear Mrs. LaRue: Letters from Obedience School* is an excellent book for modeling the think-aloud strategy, an important tool for making the invisible process of reading comprehension visible. Students will understand that reading is an active process and make inferences while reading.

Materials
- a copy of *Dear Mrs. LaRue: Letters from Obedience School* by Mark Teague
- teacher-selected text and questions for additional practice; a sample from Edgar Allan Poe's *The Oval Portrait* is provided

Procedures
1. Read the text aloud, stopping occasionally to ask the students questions. Make sure that all students can see the pictures, as the illustrations in this book are wonderful. (Ask the questions in a rhetorical manner, or pause long enough for the students to share their answers.)

   Sample Questions:
   - What did Ike do to Mrs. LaRue's chicken pot pie?
     (See the October 2 postcard.)
   - What happened between Ike and Mrs. Hibbins's cats?
     (See the October 3 postcard.)
   - How do Mrs. LaRue's neighbors feel about Ike?
     (See the October 6 postcard.)
   - How does Ike's experience change him? (See the October 11 postcard.)

   Explain that good readers think about and question the text while they read, which helps them comprehend what the author is saying. Answer any questions that the students might have.

2. Assign each student a partner and a new text, one that you have selected and prepared with stopping points for discussion. A sample is provided using Edgar Allan Poe's *The Oval Portrait.*

3. Instruct students to take turns reading. They are to stop at the designated spots to respond to or generate a question.

4. Move through the class listening as the pairs read and share. Facilitate higher-level questioning.

Extensions

- As students become more comfortable with this learning strategy, remove some of the structure. During subsequent reading sessions, omit the designated stopping points, but consider assigning a specific number of questions for the students to ask and answer. As they progress even further, remove all guidelines, and ask the students to use sticky notes to indicate where they have stopped and what question they asked at that point. In higher grades, instruct students to move toward questions that are higher on Bloom's taxonomy.
- As an assessment idea, consider turning student-generated questions into the test items. In early stages, you could do this by having students turn in their question and answer sheets. In later stages, collect their sticky note strips.

The Oval Portrait
Edgar Allan Poe

THE CHATEAU into which my valet had ventured to make forcible entrance, rather than permit me, in my desperately wounded condition, to pass a night in the open air, was one of those piles of commingled gloom and grandeur which have so long frowned among the Appennines, not less in fact than in the fancy of Mrs. Radcliffe. To all appearance it had been temporarily and very lately abandoned. We established ourselves in one of the smallest and least sumptuously furnished apartments. It lay in a remote turret of the building. Its decorations were rich, yet tattered and antique. Its walls were hung with tapestry and bedecked with manifold and multiform armorial trophies, together with an unusually great number of very spirited modern paintings in frames of rich golden arabesque. In these paintings, which depended from the walls not only in their main surfaces, but in very many nooks which the bizarre architecture of the chateau rendered necessary—in these paintings my incipient delirium, perhaps, had caused me to take deep interest; so that I bade Pedro to close the heavy shutters of the room- since it was already night—to light the tongues of a tall candelabrum which stood by the head of my bed- and to throw open far and wide the fringed curtains of black velvet which enveloped the bed itself. I wished all this done that I might resign myself, if not to sleep, at least alternately to the contemplation of these pictures, and the perusal of a small volume which had been found upon the pillow, and which purported to criticise and describe them.

<STOP>

Long—long I read—and devoutly, devotedly I gazed. Rapidly and gloriously the hours flew by and the deep midnight came. The position of the candelabrum displeased me, and outreaching my hand with difficulty, rather than disturb my slumbering valet, I placed it so as to throw its rays more fully upon the book.

But the action produced an effect altogether unanticipated. The rays of the numerous candles (for there were many) now fell within a niche of the room which had hitherto been thrown into deep shade by one of the bed-posts. I thus saw in vivid light a picture all unnoticed before. It was the portrait of a young girl just ripening into womanhood. I glanced at the painting hurriedly, and then closed my eyes. Why I did this was not at first apparent even to my own perception. But while my lids remained thus shut, I ran over in my mind my reason for so shutting them. It was an impulsive movement to gain time for thought—to make sure that my vision had not deceived me—to calm and subdue my fancy for a more sober and more certain gaze. In a very few moments I again looked fixedly at the painting.

That I now saw aright I could not and would not doubt; for the first flashing of the candles upon that canvas had seemed to dissipate the dreamy stupor which was stealing over my senses, and to startle me at once into waking life.

<STOP>

The portrait, I have already said, was that of a young girl. It was a mere head and shoulders, done in what is technically termed a vignette manner; much in the style of the favorite heads of Sully. The arms, the bosom, and even the ends of the radiant hair melted imperceptibly into the vague yet deep shadow which formed the back-ground of the whole. The frame was oval, richly gilded and filigreed in Moresque. As a thing of art nothing could be more admirable than the painting itself. But it could have been neither the execution of the work, nor the immortal beauty of the countenance, which had so suddenly and so vehemently moved me. Least of all, could it have been that my fancy, shaken from its half slumber, had mistaken the head for that of a living person. I saw at once that the peculiarities of the design, of the vignetting, and of the frame, must have instantly dispelled such idea- must have prevented even its momentary entertainment. Thinking earnestly upon these points, I remained, for an hour perhaps, half sitting, half reclining, with my vision riveted upon the portrait. At length, satisfied with the true secret of its effect, I fell back within the bed. I had found the spell of the picture in an absolute life-likeliness of expression, which, at first startling, finally confounded, subdued, and appalled me. With deep and reverent awe I replaced the candelabrum in its former position. The cause of my deep agitation being thus shut from view, I sought eagerly the volume which discussed the paintings and their histories. Turning to the number which designated the oval portrait, I there read the vague and quaint words which follow:

"She was a maiden of rarest beauty, and not more lovely than full of glee. And evil was the hour when she saw, and loved, and wedded the painter. He, passionate, studious, austere, and having already a bride in his Art; she a maiden of rarest beauty, and not more lovely than full of glee; all light and smiles, and frolicsome as the young fawn; loving and cherishing all things; hating only the Art which was her rival; dreading only the pallet and brushes and other untoward instruments which deprived her of the countenance of her lover.

\<STOP\>

It was thus a terrible thing for this lady to hear the painter speak of his desire to portray even his young bride. But she was humble and obedient, and sat meekly for many weeks in the dark, high turret-chamber where the light dripped upon the pale canvas only from overhead. But he, the painter, took glory in his work, which went on from hour to hour, and from day to day. And he was a passionate, and wild, and moody man, who became lost in reveries; so that he would not see that the light which fell so ghastly in that lone turret withered the health and the spirits of his bride, who pined visibly to all but him. Yet she smiled on and still on, uncomplainingly, because she saw that the painter (who had high renown) took a fervid and burning pleasure in his task, and wrought day and night to depict her who so loved him, yet who grew daily more dispirited and weak. And in sooth some who beheld the portrait spoke of its resemblance in low words, as of a mighty marvel, and a proof not less of the power of the painter than of his deep love for her whom he depicted so surpassingly well.

\<STOP\>

But at length, as the labor drew nearer to its conclusion, there were admitted none into the turret; for the painter had grown wild with the ardor of his work, and turned his eyes from canvas merely, even to regard the countenance of his wife. And he would not see that the tints which he spread upon the canvas were drawn from the cheeks of her who sat beside him. And when many weeks had passed, and but little remained to do, save one brush upon the mouth and one tint upon the eye, the spirit of the lady again flickered up as the flame within the socket of the lamp. And then the brush was given, and then the tint was placed; and, for one moment, the painter stood entranced before the work which he had wrought; but in the next, while he yet gazed, he grew tremulous and very pallid, and aghast, and crying with a loud voice, 'This is indeed Life itself!' turned suddenly to regard his beloved: She was dead!"

My Thoughts on *The Oval Portrait*

At each designated stopping point in the text, you and your partner will need to answer a question. If a specific question is not provided, generate an appropriate question for that section as well as possible answers.

Question 1: What kind of tone does the description of the setting establish? Use specific words and phrases in your answer(s).

Answer(s):

Question 2: What do you think the narrator may have seen that caused his alarm? Explain your answer.

Answer(s):

Question 3:

Answer(s):

Question 4:

Answer(s):

Making Inferences and Reading Comprehension

At the end of this lesson, students should be able to make and defend inferences and predictions using textual evidence.

Sheep in Wolves' Clothing by Satoshi Kitamura

This comical and wonderfully illustrated book is worth the read simply because it is fun! Packed with silliness, this book's unique text structure could be a lesson by itself. It is an ideal book for a guided reading exercise and an enjoyable introduction to any larger piece from the mystery/suspense genre.

Materials
- one or more copies of *Sheep in Wolves' Clothing* by Satoshi Kitamura
- "Guided Reading" cards (A master copy is provided; copy it on cardstock and have the students record their answers on notebook paper so that you only have to create a class set.)

Procedures
1. Based on how many copies of the book you were able to obtain, prepare the students for the reading. If you have only one copy, the lesson will be whole-class instruction with each student working independently. If you have multiple copies, the students can work in small groups; select a reader in each group.

2. Give all the students a "Before Reading" card, and have them answer the two questions.

3. Give all the students a "During Reading" card, and instruct them to address each question as they come to that point of the story. The questions are in chronological order. If students are working in groups, make sure the reader also answers the questions. Groups may read at different paces; have the reader raise his or her hand when the group has finished the book.

4. Give all the students an "After Reading" card, and have them answer the four questions.

5. When all the students are finished reading, tell them to partner up with one or two other people from another group and compare answers.

6. Facilitate a discussion about the reading. Make sure the students understand the following points:
   - Reading implies understanding, not just saying the words.
   - A good reader knows when he or she has stopped understanding.
   - It is normal for your mind to wander sometimes while you are reading.
   - It is important to know what to do when you realize you've stopped understanding what you're reading.
   - A good reader is willing to reread the parts he or she didn't understand.

- A good reader knows that one way to improve his or her understanding is to ask questions while reading.
- A good reader interacts with the text, before, during, and after reading.

Extensions
- For the next piece your students read, have them create Guided Reading cards. Use some of their questions to assess their efforts.
- Work with other content areas to create interdisciplinary lessons that utilize "Guided Reading" cards and analyze text structure.
- Use this children's book to introduce a larger mystery or suspense piece, such as a mystery by Agatha Christie or about Sherlock Holmes or any of Roald Dahl's suspense stories.

Before Reading:

1. Look at the title <u>Sheep in Wolves' Clothing</u>. Does this remind you of anything?

2. Can you make any predictions about the story based on the title?

After Reading:

1. Did you like this story? Why or why not?

2. Was it different from other children's books you've read? If so, in what way(s)?

3. Look back at the predictions you made in items 4, 8, 10, and 12 in the "During Reading" section. How many of your predictions were proven accurate by the text?

4. Into what literary genre would you classify this story?

During Reading:

1. Based on the first two pages, which literary element is obviously being used in this text?

2. Look at the line *"I love the feel of the wind fluffing my wool."* How do we as humans typically express this sentiment?

3. Look at the text structure being utilized, specifically the placement of illustrations and text. How is it different from "typical" books? Do you find it at all troublesome? Why might the author have chosen this text structure?

4. Summarize the wolves' first encounter with the sheep. Do you believe that the wolves have good intentions? Why or why not?

5. Analyze the author's choice and purpose in adding occasional dialogue to the story.

6. Why do you think the author included the lines, *"There are quite a few wolves in town.... Most of them are up to no good and play golf."?*

7. What is rugby? Is it indeed always played *"all tangled up"?*

8. Why do you think Elliott invited the cats to come along?

9. What purpose does it serve to identify the wolves' office as being in a *"seedy building"?*

10. Based on the title of the wolves' company, *"Wolfgang & Bros. Quality Knitwear,"* why do you think the wolves stole the sheep's clothing?

11. Look closely at the pictures of the fight between the wolves, cats, and sheep. Do you see anything that surprises you?

12. What do you think is in the large bag?

13. What does Hubert mean when he says, *"And these will do for now"?*

Narrative Structure and Plot

At the end of this lesson, students should be able to identify all the parts of a plot and discuss how all of those elements are needed to create a complete story.

Daddy Goose Treasury by Vivian French

We all heard nursery rhymes as children, and many of us remember them today. This lesson will examine how author Vivian French took advantage of simple rhymes to develop a complete story with carefully outlined plots. Students understand that all good stories must have a beginning, middle, and end, but some find difficulty in identifying all the parts of a good plot: exposition (basic situation), rising action (driven by conflict, both internal and external), turning point (some like to call it the climax), the falling action, and the resolution.

Materials
- a copy of *Daddy Goose Treasury* by Vivian French
- a copy of *Mother Goose Nursery Rhymes*
- several copies of different nursery rhymes (or project them, since they aren't that long)
- a copy of a plot diagram (one can easily be found online or you may use the one in the next lesson)
- a copy of the "Plot Breakdown" handout (provided) for each student

Procedures
1. Review the elements of plot with the students using the plot diagram. Give the students the "Plot Breakdown" handout and review all its parts. Help students understand that the plot diagram allows for quick delineation of the plot while the "Plot Breakdown" handout allows for expanded and more thorough coverage of the elements of the plot.

2. Read the original versions of a few nursery rhymes. Most students will be familiar with them.

3. Pick one of those nursery rhymes and ask the class to identify each part of the plot using the diagram. Write their answers on the board. Remember that they may or may not be able to identify all the parts based on the nursery rhymes you've selected.

4. Next, read the *Daddy Goose* version of one of the rhymes. Guide the class discussion, paying close attention to the fact that "Daddy" adds much more detail, thus creating a better, more richly told story. This time, the students should find it easier to identify all parts of the plot.

5. Put the students into pairs, and give them both versions of the same nursery rhyme. Give two pairs the same rhyme so they can compare them later. Have each pair use the "Plot Breakdown" handout to identify as many parts of the plot as possible in the Mother Goose version. Then have them do the same thing using the Daddy Goose version.

6. Have the students share their findings with classmates who had the same nursery rhyme. Encourage the students to discuss the similarities and differences in their findings.

7. Bring the entire group back together, and stress the importance of plot (and all of its parts) to any good story.

Extensions
- Give the students copies of the *Mother Goose Rhymes* you did not use and that are also available in the *Daddy Goose* version. Ask them to create a more complete story, incorporating all elements necessary for complete plot development.

Plot Breakdown

Title: _____

Basic Situation:
- Who are the characters?
- What is the setting?
- What is the historical context?

Rising Action:
- What are the internal conflicts?
- What are the external conflicts?
- What events lead up to the climax?

Climax:
- What is the turning point in the story?
- What is the result of the crisis?
- What is the greatest moment of tension?

Falling Action:
- What events take place after the climax?
- Why are these events important?

Resolution:
- How does everything come to an end?
- Is the major conflict resolved?

Narrative Structure and Plot

At the end of this lesson, students should be able to correctly identify the elements of a plot and apply this knowledge to a variety of narrative texts.

Fables by Arnold Lobel

Arnold Lobel's *Fables* is full of delightful, one-page morality tales that can teach a variety of literary devices. Fables are incredibly short and easy to read, making them ideal for teaching narrative structure.

Materials
- a copy of *Fables* by Arnold Lobel
- plot diagram; there are many styles, and a sample is provided
- poster paper and markers

Procedures
1. Facilitate a class discussion to introduce or review the elements of plot using the plot diagram.

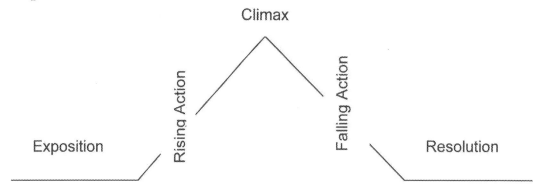

2. Read "The Bear and the Crow" on page 16.

3. Ask the students to complete a plot diagram of the fable on their own. The students should support each entry on the diagram with textual evidence.

4. Allow the students to share their plot diagram with a classmate who sits near them. Ask the partners to see if they agree on the elements of the text that complete the diagram.

5. Have the students help you complete a correct plot diagram using a projection of the template. This may generate a discussion as students lobby for their answers to be right and is also a great opportunity to correct any misunderstandings and cement the concept for struggling students.

6. As reinforcement, have the students work in small groups of three or four to complete a plot diagram for another fable. It could be another tale from this book, a classic

(perhaps Aesop), or one from James Thurber's *Fables for Our Time and Famous Poems Illustrated*. Tell the groups to transfer their completed plot diagrams to a large piece of paper (giant sticky notes or butcher paper), and display them around the room.

7. Allow the students to take a gallery walk to view the completed plot diagrams. You may want to save these to put on display for other students, school personnel, and parents to see.

Extensions
- Students can write their own fables highlighting the truism of their choice. This can spark a wonderful discussion. Collect the students' fables and create a class anthology; artistic students can assist with illustrations.
- Use "The Bear and the Crow" as an entry point to *Julius Caesar*. The commoners in the Shakespeare play are fickle and believe anything, which furthers the plans of Cassius, Brutus, and Mark Antony at different times.
- "The Bear and the Crow" also can be used as a hook for a unit on propaganda and the media. *Are consumers willing to believe anything?*

Nonction Reading, Summary and Main Idea

At the end of this lesson, students should be able to identify the main idea and create a summary of a nonfiction text.

Ruth Law Thrills a Nation by Don Brown

This short book details the cross-country flight of Ruth Law, an important event in aviation history. What a great way to remind students that nonfiction does not have to be boring! Use this book to introduce nonfiction reading, summary, and main idea.

Materials
- a copy of *Ruth Law Thrills a Nation* by Don Brown
- a copy of a short nonfiction piece of your choice (from your textbook, a textbook from another subject, a magazine, etc.)
- highlighters
- large pieces of paper (butcher paper or flip-chart paper)
- classroom art supplies

Procedures
1. As a warm-up, have the students complete a written response to the following prompt: Which do you prefer to read, fiction or nonfiction? Why?

2. Allow several volunteers to share their answers.

3. It is likely that most students will report that they prefer fiction, so be prepared to start a discussion about the importance of nonfiction. Explain that it is more than just textbooks and encyclopedias; nonfiction helps us chronicle and permanently record important events in life. Our lives are nonfiction.

4. Tell students that you're going to read about one such important event. Ask them if they have ever heard of Ruth Law. Allow any students who have to share what they know.

5. Read *Ruth Law Thrills a Nation*.

6. Ask students to turn to a partner and discuss the following questions:
   - What did you think of the book?
   - Do you think the author included too much or too little information about Ruth?

7. Ask a few students to share their answers with the entire class.

8. Point out that the author highlighted one important event in Ruth's life; he did not do a full biographical sketch. Even so, we learned a lot about Ruth and the time period in which she lived.

9. Remind the students that condensing a large amount of information is essentially what we do when we summarize and identify main ideas.

10. Distribute the short nonfiction piece you have chosen and the highlighters.

11. Model the process of identifying the main idea of each paragraph or section; do this out loud. Have a volunteer read the passage, and then allow the class to come to consensus on the main idea. They should highlight the text and write notes in the margin during the reading and discussion.

12. When the whole piece has been read, put the students in groups of three and have them review their notes so they can write a summary of the piece as a whole.

13. Tell each group to write their summary on a large piece of paper, and post it in the room.

14. Have the students participate in a gallery walk to read all the summaries.

15. As a class, decide which summary is the best one. Make sure that all the students understand *why* that summary is the best.

Extensions
- Have the students apply what they have learned by doing a mini-research project on the topic of their choice. You may want to limit the number of sources required to five or less. The students should use the information they find to generate a one-to-two page paper. From there, they can use the same process used in the activity above to pick out the main ideas and create a PowerPoint presentation, story map, or illustrated timeline.

Parallelism

At the end of this lesson, students should be able to recognize and evaluate the effects of parallel structure in literature.

This Is the Dream by Diane Z. Shore and Jessica Alexander

This poignant book highlights life before and after the civil rights movement. It is ideal for teaching parallel structure and introducing literature about the struggle for equality in America.

Materials
- a copy of *This Is the Dream* by Diane Z. Shore and Jessica Alexander
- examples of "before" and "after" pictures, such as those in advertisements for weight loss and makeovers, photos of a city before and after a natural disaster, yearbook and current pictures of celebrities, or pictures of your city fifty years ago and as it is today
- pens and paper for the students

Procedures
1. Show the students several examples of "before" and "after" pictures, and ask them to identify the differences between the two.

2. Ask the students to write about one of the examples you have shown them. Their short pieces should detail what the person, city, etc., looked like "before" and what it looked like "after."

3. Read *This Is the Dream* to the class.

4. Point out to the students the authors' use of parallelism, and have them discuss its effect on the reader.

5. Tell the students to return to their short written pieces and revise them to improve the parallel structure. They should imitate Shore and Alexander's use of the technique.

6. Ask the students to read their finished products aloud to a partner or small group.

7. For closure, have students write on small slips of paper what they learned about parallelism from the day's activity. Use this feedback to revisit the topic if necessary.

Extensions
- Have the students write a longer "before and after" process paper. They can tackle a historical event, an event from their own lives, or return to the media for inspiration.
- Use this book to introduce longer literary pieces focusing on the civil rights movement or racial inequality. Suggestions include:
  - *A Lesson Before Dying*, by Ernest Gaines
  - *Cry, the Beloved Country*, by Alan Paton
  - *I Know Why the Caged Bird Sings*, by Maya Angelou
  - *To Kill a Mockingbird*, by Harper Lee

Parody

At the end of this lesson, students should be able to identify and describe a parody as well as create their own parodies.

One Dark and Dreadful Night by Randy Cecil

One Dark and Dreadful Night parodies three well-known children's stories with a little added flair ... and bunnies. This humorous book is an excellent resource for teaching the concept of parody. The added bonus is the silly dialogue that provides a secondary plot.

Materials
- a copy of *One Dark and Dreadful Night* by Randy Cecil
- copies of various fairy tales
- classroom art supplies
- pens and paper for the students

Procedures
1. Introduce the concept of parody, and let students know that parodies abound.

2. Ask students to identify their favorite childhood story or fairy tale.

3. Compile a list on the board. You may choose to write it, or select a student to act as a scribe, or invite students to come up and add their favorite to the list.

4. Tell the students that they will hear three well-known fairy tales: "A Wolf in the Woods of Woe," "The Beans of Doom," and "Lost in Foggy Forest." Give the students the opportunity to guess the actual fairy tales being parodied based on these titles.

5. Read *One Dark and Dreadful Night*. Be sure to read the actors' ongoing dialogue as well.

6. Now that the students have seen a model, tell them to write a parody of their previously identified favorite fairy tale. It is fine if several students work with the same fairy tale; their products should be very different. You may also choose to let the students to work in pairs.

7. Encourage the students to create their storyline before they attempt to add dialogue and illustrations.

8. Once students have completed their parodies, allow them to share their work with the class. You can do this in a variety of ways.
   - End each class period with a few "guest authors" reading their stories from an "author's chair."
   - With large classes and if there are time constraints, organize the students in groups of four, and have them share their stories with their group.
   - Put the finished pieces on display for a few weeks.

Extensions
- After demonstrating proficiency in creating a parody of a fairy tale, encourage the students to tackle a larger literary work, such as a Shakespeare piece.

Personification

At the end of this lesson, students should be able to discuss how personification can be used to highlight certain elements of a story.

Sylvester and the Magic Pebble by William Steig

Many children's stories are written with animals as the main characters, yet some students find personification challenging to understand. This tale of a little boy who loses his way helps children see that almost anything can take on humanlike traits, which is the primary principle of personification. *Sylvester and the Magic Pebble* also provides an opportunity to explore satire with the class.

Materials
- a copy of *Sylvester and the Magic Pebble* by William Steig
- a dry-erase board or chalk board
- pens and paper for the students

Procedures
1. Help the students understand the concept of personification and have a working definition of it. To evaluate their comprehension of the concept, spend a few minutes allowing the students to give their own definitions and examples.

2. Inform the students that you are going to read a story to them. Ask them to listen closely and make a list of all the different things they think are being personified on a sheet of paper.

3. After you have finished reading the story, ask the students to count the total number of items they have listed as personified.

4. Allow the students to compare their numbers. More than likely, there will be several different numbers, which should lead to a discussion.

5. After the students have had some time to share their findings, put all the different personified items on the board, and have the students write them down.

6. Ask the students to explain how each item is an example of personification and the possible effects that it had on the story. Initiate a class discussion.

7. Once students have completed this task, read the story again, and ask students to make a list of anything in the story that was *not* personified but could have been.

8. Have the students speculate on why the author chose not to personify these items. (The goal is to allow students to see that not everything needs to "come to life" in a story, but sometimes the author's decision to use personification greatly enhances the story.)

Extensions
- Ask the students to choose an item that was not personified in the story. Then they should write to another character as though they have been "magically brought to life" by the author for the sole purpose of communicating a very important fact or message that was left out of the original text.

Point of View

At the end of this lesson, students should be able to examine how multiple characters can present the same story in different ways, which is the concept of point of view.

Ira Sleeps Over by Bernard Waber

Bernard Waber uses one little boy, his well-meaning parents, and his annoying older sister to present a warm tale of the planning involved in a child's very first sleepover, especially when a "special" friend is involved. *Ira Sleeps Over* explores the different perspectives of all the characters involved, which allows students to see how points of view—of both the speaker and the listener—greatly influence the meaning of the overall story.

Materials
- a copy of the book *Ira Sleeps Over* by Bernard Waber
- a copy of the "Four Square Perspective" handout (provided) for each student

Procedures
1. Ask the students if they remember their first sleepover. Ask them to recall what they most looked forward to and of what they were most scared. Did their parents and siblings encourage them or make them even more scared? After the discussion is over, inform the students that as you read the book, they should analyze each character's perspective about the event that is about to take place. (This activity also could be done as a warm-up or journal entry.)

2. Read only a portion of the book to the students. Stop at the part where the sister asks, "What if Reggie wants to know your teddy bear's name? Did you think about that?" Read to the bottom of that page, and stop.

3. Have a quick debate with your students about whether Ira should take his bear. Put the students' positions on the board, if you choose.

4. Ask the students to consider how each character (Mom, Dad, Sister, Reggie, Ira) feels about taking a bear to a sleepover.

5. Give the students the "Four Square Perspective" handout and instruct them to put the words "Bringing a teddy bear to your first sleepover" in the center box. Have them put a character's name in each quadrant. (To make your assessment easier or to check for understanding, have the students label all the quadrants in the same order.)

6. In the "Different Perspectives" section, have the students write the words: "Should Ira take a teddy bear to his first sleepover?"

7. Give the students time to fill in each quadrant with the character's justification of why Ira should or should not take the bear. Guide them through one to make sure they understand the process. You may want to have students identify textual support for their observations. *Important:* Tell students not to complete the bottom portion of the handout.

8. After the students have completed the quadrants (either individually or in small groups), direct their attention to the bottom portion of the handout. Give them sentence stems to help them fill in this section, for example:
    - Based on (a certain character's) reactions or comments, I think that ...
    - This situation is similar to ...
    - A question that I have is ...
    - I believe the characters act this way or say the things they do because ...

9. Wrap up the lesson by informing the class that point of view can change both a story's presentation and its outcome.

Extensions
- Have the students assume the role of the teddy bear and write a letter to one of the main characters. The bear should state how he feels about what was said to Ira when he was trying to make his decision. This activity will help focus the students on voice, especially if you instruct them to think about whether or not the bear was angry, happy, sad, anxious, excited, etc.

Four Square Perspective

Different Perspectives on:

_____

_____

Character One:	Character Two:
Character Three:	Character Four:

Conclusions/Connections/Questions...

Point of View

At the end of this lesson, students should be able to recognize different points of view and evaluate how different points of view affect the telling of a story.

Joyful Noise: Poems for Two Voices by Paul Fleischman

This is a beautiful book of poetry that explores its content from various perspectives. It is meant to be read by pairs of readers, each one taking a different point of view.

Materials
- a copy of the book *Joyful Noise: Poems for Two Voices* by Paul Fleischman
- dry-erase board and markers, document camera, or the like
- a film clip that utilizes a unique point of view, such as *A Bug's Life* or *Toy Story*

Procedures
1. Show the students the film clip, and facilitate a discussion on the importance of point of view.

2. Ask the students to read several excerpts from *Joyful Noise*.

3. Allow students to share their thoughts on the poems and discuss the effect that hearing two perspectives had on them as readers.

4. Have students create their own poems for two voices.

5. Invite volunteers to write their poems on a projection device, and read them aloud. Or divide the class into two halves, and do a choral reading.

6. Have the students use the activity as a springboard for a larger piece of writing. For example, ask them to:
   - Rewrite a very short story—such as *The Story of an Hour* by Kate Chopin or *The Oval Portrait* by Edgar Allan Poe—from another character's point of view.
   - Draw from a container the names of the characters in a literary work—one the class is reading or has just finished reading. Then each student should create a journal for his or her character, retelling events in the story from that point of view.

Extensions
- Since this lesson blends very easily into a lesson on personification, allow students to write about a day in the life of an object (e.g., My Life as an Alarm Clock).

Point of View

At the end of this lesson, students should be able to identify specific points of view and discuss the effect they have on how a story is told.

The True Story of the 3 Little Pigs by Jon Scieszka

It's interesting to hear the same story told from two perspectives. This cute story allows us to examine different aspects of narration through Jon Scieszka's retelling of a classic from the point of view of a character who believes he's been wronged: the wolf. With this text, a teacher can introduce or review the different vantage points from which a story can be told as well as help students examine how a person's perspective can change everything.

Materials
- a copy of *The True Story of the 3 Little Pigs* by Jon Scieszka
- a copy of the original story "The Three Little Pigs"
- pens and paper for the students

Procedures
1. Review the different types of point of view. Be sure that students know the problems certain points of view can cause (e.g., the lack of plausibility created by an unreliable narrator).

2. Read the original story to the students to refresh students' memories and introduce the story to those who are unfamiliar with it. Next, read the Scieszka version, and instruct the students to take notes about the differences between the two versions of the story.

3. Discuss with the entire class how the stories differ. Have a student list the differences on the board in the form of a T-chart: the wolf's story versus the original story. Guide the students in their thinking by pointing out some of the things the wolf says that seem skewed. Ask the students why they suppose the wolf says these things and how much they believe his story.

4. Have students work individually to find clues in the story that suggest that the wolf may not be telling the truth. After about ten minutes, have them share their findings with a partner, discussing the objectivity of the narrator. Be sure to point out things you discussed in your earlier discussion about point of view.

Extensions
- Have the students pick another character that was involved in the story (e.g., one of the pig's brothers), and retell the story from his point of view.

Pronoun Usage

At the end of this lesson, students will be able to identify nonspecific pronouns and create more effective antecedents.

The Fungus that Ate My School by Arthur Dorros

Kids have wonderful imaginations when it comes to science and scientific processes. This story provides a cute examination of how children view fungus while allowing for the study of pronouns and antecedents.

Materials
- a copy of *The Fungus that Ate My School* by Arthur Dorros
- handouts of pre-selected excerpts from the book for a group activity
- a dry-erase board or chalk board

Procedures
1. Inform the class that you will introduce (or give a quick review of) common pronouns. Ask the class to list some pronouns. Write their responses on the board.

2. Before reading the story, ask the students to note how many times they hear "it" or "its" in the story. Read the story. Have students share how many times they heard "it" or "its."

3. Place the students into groups or pairs and give them the excerpts you have selected. It is okay if more than one group has the same excerpt; they will most likely generate different answers. Put the example below on the board, and address it with the class.

   Original sentence: "It started before spring vacation."
   Revised sentence: "The <u>mysterious growth</u> started before spring vacation."

Explain how the picture has been "painted" for the reader, providing more understanding of what is being discussed.

4. Do one or two more examples together if needed. Then have the groups rewrite their assigned excerpts replacing the pronouns "it" and "its" with nouns or noun phrases. If more than one group has the same excerpt, allow time for them to discuss the different descriptions they used to replace the pronouns.

5. Come back to a large group setting and read the story again, allowing the pairs or groups to insert their revisions when you come to their assigned sections.

6. Close the lesson by reiterating the importance of being specific when writing. Be sure that students understand that using too many pronouns can confuse the reader.

Extensions
- Find several copies of flash fiction (very short stories) or simple children's texts, and have the students replace the major nouns with pronouns. After they turn in their assignments, pass them out to small groups, and see if they can correctly identify the original nouns.

Satire

At the end of this lesson, students should be able to discuss their feelings about standardized testing and analyze the purpose of satire.

Hooray for Diffendoofer Day by Dr. Seuss with some help from Jack Prelutsky and Lane Smith

This posthumous Dr. Seuss (Theodor Geisel) book tackles standardized testing in the way only Dr. Seuss could. Use it to introduce satire while easing student tension around test time.

Materials
- a copy of *Hooray for Diffendoofer Day* by Dr. Seuss with Jack Prelutsky and Lane Smith
- pens and paper for the students

Procedures
1. Facilitate a class discussion that allows the students to share their feelings about standardized testing.

2. Read *Hooray for Diffendoofer Day*.

3. Have students respond to the text in writing, identifying any correlations they see between the book and their school, city, or state, as well as why they think the author wrote the book.

4. Allow the students to share their written responses.

5. Remind the students that, just like the students in the book, they know what they need to know to do well on any test.

6. Introduce the concept of satire, and have the students discuss how Dr. Seuss satirizes standardized testing and the public school system.

Extensions
- Have students to choose their own social issue and write a satirical piece about it.
- Use this exercise to introduce a larger, satirical literary piece, such as *Animal Farm* (George Orwell).
- Discuss Dr. Seuss's role as a social commentator and his use of satire. Suggestions for additional Seuss books to include in this exercise:
  - *The Butter Battle Book*, which addresses war and the nuclear arms race
  - *The Lorax*, which addresses environmental issues
  - *The Sneetches*, which addresses racism and social equality
  - *Yertle the Turtle*, which addresses tyranny and political activism

Setting Analysis

At the end of the lesson, students should be able to identify several components that establish the setting of a story and explain how those components contribute to the tone.

Pearl Moscowitz's Last Stand by Arthur A. Levine

Students often have a tendency to read through a story and not really pay close attention to the setting. Sure, most students can tell you that setting means "time and place," but few explore beyond that. This story allows students to see how setting can greatly change not only the characters but also the meaning behind the story. Pearl Moscowitz is a woman who has seen many things over the years, and she realizes that there comes a time when we must all stand up for what we believe.

Materials
- a copy of *Pearl Moscowitz's Last Stand* by Arthur A. Levine
- a copy of the "Tools for Analyzing Setting" handout (provided) for each student

Procedures
1. Read the book to the students, stopping to ask guiding questions:
   - What is so unique about Pearl's name? What does her last name possibly indicate about her background?
   - How many years seem to have passed between the beginning and ending of the book?
   - What's so special about all the different people that move into Pearl's neighborhood?
   - What message do you think the author is trying to get across? (You may have to help students answer this question, which addresses theme.)

2. Ask the students to tell you what they know about setting. Make a list on the board.

3. After the list is complete, inform students that there is more to setting a scene than just describing the time and place.

4. Put the students into pairs or small groups, and give them the "Tools for Analyzing Setting" handout. Guide the students through at least one section so that you can address any questions that may arise concerning the activity.

5. Give the students sufficient time to complete the handout. You may choose to assign each section to one or two groups or assign roles in each group to make sure everyone stays on task.

6. Once everyone is finished, bring the class back together for a group discussion. Ask the students to offer their thoughts on why one answer or observation is more accurate than another. Modify the charts, as appropriate.

7. After the charts have been updated and there is no more relevant discussion, ask the students to write about the setting of the story. Give them guiding questions to aid their writing:
   - Does the author do a good job of creating a believable setting?
   - What would have made the setting more realistic?
   - What could the author have left out in creating the setting?
   - What is the one thing you can't believe the author forgot to include in the description of the setting?

Extensions
   - This strategy could easily be modified for use at the beginning of a longer piece that the students will study where different scenes and the setting as a whole affect the storyline. Suggestions include:
     o *The Outsiders*, by S.E. Hinton
     o *Lord of the Flies*, by William Golding
     o *Holes*, by Louis Sachar

Tools for Analyzing Setting

Title: _____   Author: _____

Questions to consider		Observations from the story
1. **What is the setting?** • Is there a specific historical period indicated? • Do we know the time of day? • What is the weather like? • Is there anything that looks interesting? Smells funny? • Are there particular sounds that you are aware of? • Is there a specific country indicated?		
2. **How do the characters react to the setting?** • Is there something specific that they want from this place? • Are any of the elements of the setting acting as antagonists to the character(s)? • What are the external conflicts that the setting creates?		
3. **Can we draw any conclusions about the characters from the descriptions of the setting?** • How do the characters react to their surroundings? • What types of feelings do the characters have about the setting? (hope, disdain, joy, pain, fear, disrespect)		
4. **What type of mood does the setting help to create?** • Are situations presented in a fearful atmosphere? Suspicious? Cheery? Sinister?		

Theme: Alienation of Individuals and Groups

At the end of this lesson, students should be able to evaluate the effects of alienation on a character and apply that knowledge to other literary texts.

The Cow That Went OINK by Bernard Most

Meet the laughingstock of the barnyard, a cow that says "oink." She is ostracized by the other animals until the day she meets a pig that says "moo." Together, they create and implement a plan that gives them the last laugh. Though this book is incredibly simple, it is an excellent tool for introducing the common literary theme of alienation.

Materials
- a copy of *The Cow That Went OINK* by Bernard Most
- pens and paper for the students

Procedures
1. As a warm-up, have the students complete a written response to the following prompt: Have you ever felt like you didn't "fit in"? Describe how you felt and what you did.

2. Invite volunteers to share their responses. (Please note that some students may become emotional. Encourage them to continue and commend their courage for sharing.)

3. Read *The Cow That Went OINK* to the class.

4. Facilitate a class discussion about the repercussions of alienating a person or a group. (Make sure that the class understands the rules for effective discussion.)

5. Use this discussion to introduce a larger literary work that incorporates the theme of alienation. Suggestions include:
   - *A Stranger in the Village*, a short story by James Baldwin
   - *The Handsomest Drowned Man in the World*, a short story by Gabriel Garcia Marquez
   - *Lord of the Flies*, a novel by William Golding
   - *One Day in the Life of Ivan Denisovich*, a novel by Alexander Solzhenitsyn

Extensions
- This discussion can lead to a variety of writing assignments, such as:
   - a personal narrative that develops the experience shared in the warm-up
   - a research composition on a topic related to alienation or bullying
   - a persuasive essay in which students justify or oppose alienating an individual or a group

Theme: Fear of the Unknown

At the end of this lesson, students should be able to recognize and analyze thematic links to the common social issues of intolerance and the fear of the unknown.

The Widow's Broom by Chris Van Allsburg

This rather unusual children's book explores what happens when witches' brooms lose their powers. One broom finds happiness with a widow. *The Widow's Broom* is ideal for discussing a common human phenomenon and literary theme—fear of the unknown.

Materials
- a copy of *The Widow's Broom* by Chris Van Allsburg
- a DVD of *Beauty and the Beast* or a recording of "The Mob Song" from the soundtrack of *Beauty and the Beast*
- pens and paper for the students

Procedures
1. As a warm-up, have the students complete a written response to the following prompt: Why do you think people are afraid of the unknown or people and things that are different?

2. Ask volunteers to share their responses, and use their answers to facilitate a class discussion on the issue. Be prepared for some interesting answers. With older, more mature students, you can delve deeper by bringing up the issue of hate crimes and real-life examples of people ostracizing or harming individuals who are different.

3. Show the clip from *Beauty and the Beast* where Gaston incites the townspeople to kill the beast. Or play "The Mob Song" from the movie soundtrack. Ask students to listen closely to the dialogue or the lyrics. Play the piece several times if necessary. Make certain they cue in on the parts that show the townspeople are afraid of things they don't understand.

4. Based on the class discussion of their warm-up and the song, have students write a well-constructed paragraph describing why they think so many literary works explore the theme of humanity's fear of the unknown.

5. Challenge students to evaluate both their own and society's levels of tolerance and acceptance as they read a longer piece. Suggestions include:
   - *Dandelion Wine*, by Ray Bradbury
   - *Frankenstein*, by Mary Shelley
   - *Lord of the Flies*, by William Golding
   - *The Crucible*, by Arthur Miller
   - *The Metamorphosis*, by Franz Kafka

Extensions
- This is an excellent source for introducing the genres of suspense or science fiction. For example, your class might complete this activity before reading the short story *Harrison Bergeron* by Kurt Vonnegut.
- Have students complete a persuasive writing piece on the following topic: Was the widow right to lie to her neighbors?

Theme: Personal Sacrifice and Goal Attainment

At the end of this lesson, students should be able to recognize a thematic link between two genres of literature and discuss pursuing a dream as a common literary theme.

Uncle Jed's Barbershop by Margaree King Mitchell

This book is Sarah Jean's tribute to her Uncle Jedediah, the only black barber in the county in the early 1900s. In describing his lifelong goal of opening his own barbershop, Sarah Jean takes us through some difficult times in American history. *Uncle Jed's Barbershop* can be used in many ways and ties in well with any unit about goals, dreams, or personal sacrifices and triumphs.

Materials
- a copy of *Uncle Jed's Barbershop* by Margaree King Mitchell
- a copy of the poem "Dream Deferred" by Langston Hughes
- pens and paper for the students

Procedures
1. Ask students to list two to five of their dreams and goals. Then ask them to identify how many years they are willing to work to achieve those dreams and goals.

2. Invite a few volunteers to share their responses.

3. Read *Uncle Jed's Barbershop.*

4. Facilitate a class discussion that incorporates the following questions:
    - What was Uncle Jed's goal?
    - How long did it take him to reach his goal?
    - What kind of setbacks did he face along the way?
    - How did Uncle Jed deal with those setbacks?
    - What do you think Sarah Jean learned from Uncle Jed?
    - What can we learn from Uncle Jed?

5. Remind the students that perseverance toward a goal is a common theme in literature.

6. Project the Langston Hughes poem and read it to the class.

7. Ask the students to write a well-constructed paragraph in which they respond to the poem and explain how the poem and the story are similar.

8. Invite a few volunteers to share their responses.

9. Lead a discussion about how the two authors used different genres to highlight a similar theme. Encourage the students to think about and discuss other literature they have read that shares the same theme.

Extensions
- Use this lesson as an introduction to a longer literary piece with a similar theme, such as *A Raisin in the Sun* (Lorraine Hansberry) or *A Tale of Two Cities* (Charles Dickens).
- Have the students expand their responses to Hughes's poem into longer pieces, such as an interpretive response or literary analysis.

Theme: Quest for Fame and Fortune

At the end of this lesson, students should be able to use textual evidence to identify and support a theme.

Cat, You Better Come Home by Garrison Keillor

Follow Puff the cat as she leaves home to find a place where she is appreciated and where all her dreams can come true. Though she spends time in the lap of luxury, she eventually discovers who her real friends are. *Cat, You Better Come Home* is a teacher's treasure trove, filled with rich vocabulary and wonderful imagery and packed with life lessons. Use this lesson to introduce any literary work that focuses on an individual's quest for fame and fortune.

Materials
- a copy of *Cat, You Better Come Home* by Garrison Keillor
- pens and paper for the students
- quote strips; see below for suggested quotes

Procedures
1. As a warm-up, have the students complete a written response to the following questions:
   - When you were little, did you ever think about running away from home? Why?
   - Where did you plan to go?
   - How long were you planning to stay away?
   - Did you tell your parents? If so, how did they respond to your plans?
   - If you never thought about running away, write about a place you would like to visit or live, and explain why.

   Allow a few volunteers to share their responses.

2. Read *Cat, You Better Come Home* to the class, asking students to listen and make notes when they hear something amusing, poignant, or otherwise interesting. They should also make note of any words they hear but do not understand. A list of words that may be new to the students appears below in order of their appearance in the book.

highbrow	promenade
paté	abyss
sardonic	skids (slang)
stole (noun)	ragout
manse	flambé
entourage	muscatel
minions	status quo

3. Have the students share their notes with partners or in small groups. They should help each other define the words they do not know. If certain words are new to the majority of the class, post those on the board and ask volunteers to look them up in the dictionary and post the definitions. Before the students copy the meanings into their notebooks, review the list and help them obtain a working definition of each term.

4. Divide the class into nine groups, and assign each one a quote from the text to analyze, both for its relevance to the rest of the book and to life. (Print and laminate the quotes on cardstock to improve their longevity.) Here are some suggestions (from the 1995 edition of the book) for the quote strips:
   - page 13, last three lines
   - page 17, last two lines
   - page 20, last three lines
   - page 24, all four lines
   - page 25, four lines in center of page
   - page 28, first three lines
   - page 32, first four lines
   - page 32, last two lines
   - page 33, all four lines

5. Allow each group to share its quote and the results of the discussion and analysis. This will most likely spark a lively discussion as the students discover that the book is more about them than it is about Puff.

6. Let the students know that the quest for wealth and fame is a common motif in literature.

7. Introduce the major work the class will be studying that has similar themes. Suggestions include:
   - *Great Expectations*, by Charles Dickens
   - *The Odyssey*, by Homer
   - *Wuthering Heights*, by Emily Bronte

Extensions
- To delve deeper into man's inherent need for a safe place, particularly when hardships occur, read "Storm Home" from Keillor's *News from Lake Wobegon*. Have the students write about their own "storm home," their own safe place.

Voice

At the end of this lesson, students should be able to determine how an author uses voice as well as use the R.A.F.T. technique (explained below) to develop their own voices in their writing.

A Fine, Fine School by Sharon Creech

It's too bad we didn't all have a book like this when we were younger. Sharon Creech does a wonderful job of using humor to portray a principal who thinks that too much is never enough. There is such a strong voice in this story. It begs to be interpreted and reenacted by students. Since acting is not always an option, students also can explore their voices on paper, assuming the different roles of all the characters in this story.

Materials
- a copy of *A Fine, Fine School* by Sharon Creech
- several copies of newspapers with editorial sections (or copies of several editorials)
- sticky notes (for annotations, so that students may "converse" with the text while they read)
- a copy of the "Character Profile Chart" (provided) for each student
- several large sheets of butcher paper or poster boards
- pens and paper for the students

Procedures
1. Introduce the students to the concept of an editorial. Explain that editorials offer opinions about a certain topic and often ask the reader to take some sort of action. Ask the students to read several editorials in the newspapers you've provided so that they are familiar with the format.

2. Read the story to the students, asking them to make notes of all the things with which they disagree. Discuss the illustrations and the messages the illustrators may be trying to convey, explaining that editorial comments are often made through art as well. Tell the students to write down the messages related by the pictures in the story.

3. Divide the students into groups, and ask each group to pick one character. (Younger students may prefer to choose characters from a list you provide.) After the groups have selected their characters, tell them to complete the "Character Profile Chart" as it relates to their character and then transfer that information onto a large sheet of butcher paper or a poster board.

4. Have the groups hang their posters around the room and conduct a quick gallery walk, allowing the groups to view all the characters and decide if they agree with each profile. As a class, discuss the findings of each group. If needed, have groups make adjustments to their posters.

5. Have students do another quick gallery walk, this time copying the profiles of the other characters into their "Character Profile Chart." In addition, have students think about all the different complaints each character might have and allow students to add these complaints to the bottom of each chart as they complete the gallery walk. These complaints may be written on sticky notes.

6. Have the student groups write either an editorial or a letter to the principal, in the guise of the character they've chosen, discussing a topic of their choice, perhaps related to the principal's suggestions for more school. (Some students may choose to write as the principal, defending his choice to have more school.) Remind them to refer back to the "Character Profile Chart" to make sure that the personalities of their characters stand out and to focus on the role (R) of the persona they are assuming; the audience (A) to whom they are writing; the format (F) they choose to use for their communication; and their chosen topic (T)—this is the R.A.F.T. technique.

Extensions
- Have the students create an editorial cartoon of a current event. (You may want to create a list of current events from which they can choose.) Several students are likely to choose the same issue. Depending on how many students and issues you have, combine the different submissions and create a gallery walk. Then ask the students to determine whether the cartoon is for or against the issue.

Character Profile Chart

Name of Character	Role the character plays in the story	Is the character presented in a positive or negative role?	What are the major personality traits of this character?

A Few Final Thoughts

Secondary English/Language Arts (ELA) teachers face numerous challenges. An average day finds these teachers juggling a paper load, working to create authentic opportunities for students to write, and trying to make 150 adolescents understand the still-relevant themes of classic literature. And that's just the teaching. Then there are the deadlines, the data, the meetings, and the constantly changing technology. It's no wonder that ELA teachers can look a bit haggard by the end of a semester.

But take heart. What you do matters. The Secondary ELA classroom is an amazingly important place. It is where students transition from "learning to read" to "reading to learn," and they need a tremendous amount of guidance to make that leap. It is where they learn the comprehension and writing skills that are required for success in every other area. And, hopefully, it is where they find their voices and the confidence to try new things and take on different perspectives. Make no mistake: what happens in the ELA classroom impacts every other classroom in a child's life.

Educational leadership, buzz words, and even methods of teaching will continue to change over the years. Yet some things will never change. Our students still need the same things they have always needed: love, encouragement, and passionate teachers who are willing to invest in them. Thank you for the investment you are making in your students' lives. You never know who might be sitting in your classroom today—an innovative designer, a renowned physician, or even a future president.

We hope this book has been a useful tool for planning and energizing your classroom. We hope "story time" has gained a place in your hearts and will be a permanent part of your classroom routine. Above all, we hope that you and your students never lose the childlike awe and wonder of learning.